NOT EXACTLY AN ENDORSEMENT

I know that many authors preview their books to a small audience for the purpose of "endorsements". The goal is to share accolades from the most impressive people they know – people with recognizable names and titles, leaders of ministries, and successful authors, when possible. I also shared the earliest versions of my manuscript with a few people who are close to me, and I was grateful for their feedback. But if I'm being honest, my intentions when writing this book were not typical. I don't desire fame or fortune, I only want the Lord to get this book into the hands of those whose hearts need it most. I have felt His endorsement on it since the beginning – a heavenly stamp of approval and favor, and His gentle voice nudging me, "Keep going."

Perhaps the only "human endorsement" I needed from this project was that of the perpetrator himself. It's not that no one is more important to me, many people are. I suppose his approval is a full-circle confirmation of a few things: Yes, the story as I have told it is true and accurate. Yes, I told it in a way that honors my son's life, as well as his. Yes, this project was worth it. Worth the time, worth the effort, worth re-living some of my very worst memories. I've proven to myself that I can "go there" and not lose any of the victory I so confidently proclaim over my life since forgiving my son's killer. This project proved that radical forgiveness took over in the places that pain once ruled and that I can tell the story in its' entirety without my heart breaking all over again.

After I gave the manuscript to Pete in November of 2025, I

waited, only somewhat patiently, for his response. I have learned over the years that Pete's correspondence tends to be short, genuine and to the point: *"The book is amazing, heartfelt and honest."* I read those words, sighed in relief, and thought to myself, "OK, that's it. That's what my soul needed most." It was time to publish.

Justice and Mercy

A healed heart:
A mother's memoir of murder and miracles.

Debbi Edwards
with Shannon Musa

Unless otherwise indicated, all Scripture quotations in this publication are taken from The Holy Bible, New International Version, NIV copyright © 1973, 1978, 1984, 2011 by Biblica, Inc. Used by permission. All rights reserved worldwide.

Scripture quotations marked (NKJV) are taken from the New King James Version. Copyright © 1982 by Thomas Nelson. Used by permission. All rights reserved.

ISBN 13: 979-8-234-01677-5 (paperback)

AUTHOR'S NOTE AND DEDICATION

This book came about through a strange series of events and divine timing. How does one with a story in their heart, and a message to share, find someone to write it for them? How does one find a writer that they can entrust with the sacred story that defined almost their entire life?

After my son Eric's murder in 1991, with every year that passed it felt like less people in my life had personally known him. Through the years, I had crossed paths with a friend of his, and we remained connected on Facebook. I loosely kept up with her life to the extent that social media permitted. I knew we still lived local to each other, I knew she had a couple of sons, and I always had in the back of my mind, "She knew Eric".

In January of 2025 as I was scrolling, I read a post that caused me to reach out…"Hi Shannon. I so enjoy your posts, you have a way with words. I wish I did, I would write a book about Eric's murder and all the ways losing him changed our lives. Did I tell you that Pete is out of prison and we are in contact? I've forgiven him and dare I say we are friends? It's quite the story. Maybe someday I'll share it with you!"

The quick reply I received was, "Debbi. I would love to hear. Let's get together. Let's consider writing a book. Why not? You give me some materials and some interview time, and I'll write a test chapter. If you like it, we move on. If you hate it, we drop it. But we should at least try."

From that moment on, our hearts were knit together. We have so much in common, and Shannon's boys are the exact ages my boys were when we lost Eric. We both love the Lord, we both have Mesa, Arizona roots, and we both worry too much for too long about everything. The words began flowing, chapter by chapter, and we were so attuned there were often very few corrections to the manuscript.

We have done our best to keep this true story, "true." We have reviewed untold hours of police notes, court hearings, and keepsakes like letters, cards, and even logs of phone messages. Any mistakes are due to the passage of time and details becoming dull over the years.

This book is dedicated to my husband Paul Edwards. We have been through hell and back together, but God has been exceedingly good to us for over 54 years! To Jason, my son, being your mom has been the joy of my heart and I have so many reasons to be proud of you. To Eric, we didn't have long enough together on this earth, but thankfully, our reunion in Heaven will last forever. And to Pete, because of you, I understand the depths of forgiveness and the power of redemption. I wish nothing but the best for you.

Eric Edwards January 16, 1973-December 4, 1991

my heart woke me crying last night
how can i help i begged
my heart said
write the book
       -Rupi Kaur, *Prologue* from *Milk and Honey*

Contents

Prologue

T HEY SAY EVERYONE has a story, and I am no exception. Many people can relate to pieces of me: a chaotic and dysfunctional childhood, marrying and starting my family when I was young, 20 years in nursing, and choosing Jesus before I knew just how desperately I would need Him. These are normal and common things, stuff we could discuss on a long flight together or sitting in a crowded waiting room. A little trust between us, and just like that, these stories come spilling out. But there's more to me. There's a part of my story that doesn't come spilling out as if you can relate, because I assume you can't. Few can understand being the mother of a murdered teen. That was the pain that settled behind my eyes and in my heart for 27 years. Some may have picked up on it, but it was a depth of sorrow they wouldn't have imagined and definitely couldn't put their finger on. For the most part, it stayed within me. I'm getting older now, and it's time to tell my story. Against seemingly insurmountable odds, this story ends with forgiveness, redemption, and freedom. This story ends with friendship between me and my son's killer. It's a long and winding ride. Join me?

Owe no one anything except to love one another, for he who loves another has fulfilled the law. For the commandments, "You shall not commit adultery," "You shall not murder," "You shall not steal, "You shall not bear false witness," "You shall not covet," and if there is any other commandment, are all summed up in this saying, namely,

"You shall love your neighbor as yourself." Love does no harm to a neighbor; therefore love *is* the fulfillment of the law. *Romans 13: 8-10 NKJV*

PART ONE:

Hurt

When someone causes you pain so deep and unfair that you cannot forget it, you are pushed into the first stage of the crisis of forgiving.

Adapted from: <u>Forgive and Forget</u> by Lewis B. Smedes

1

The Beginning

NOBODY EVER TOLD me, "Debbi, nothing is for keeps. And if it's good, it won't last." I just knew it. Expected it. Husbands leave, relationships fail. Life can be so hard. Likewise, no one told me the exception to these unspoken certainties would be my children. I just knew that. Expected it. I was sure I would have my babies with me until the day I died. Even in a hectic and chaotic world, a mom is not supposed to outlive her babies.

I was born Deborah Lynn Huesmann, January 31, 1954. You can call me Debbi. Most of my life, from the best parts, to the unspeakably worst, happened in Mesa, Arizona. Drive through Mesa with me and I'll take you on a journey. See that yellow brick home? That's where my story began. The convenience store on the corner? That's right next door to an after-school hangout called Sandy's Hamburgers and it's where I met the love of my life. There is the church where I first heard about Jesus, and this is the church where I met my best friend. A few miles east and we enter the desert-turned-tract neighborhood where my son's body was found...and this is the cemetery where he lies. Good old Mesa. Wholesome on the outside, but there are skeletons in that closet.

Now, let's get back to the love of my life. His name is Paul. I was 14 and a freshman at Carson Junior High and Paul was 17 and a senior at Westwood High School. A mutual friend introduced us. It was awkward because I had no experience and Paul had lots. Paul has his own stories to tell, and he could write a book of his own, but for the purpose of helping you understand us, I'll share a bit. On one of our first dates, I was in the car with Paul and four other guys. Paul was driving and he whipped the car around in the middle of the road and all five guys jumped out of the car to confront a kid that wanted to fight Paul's younger brother. As much as it shocked me, I didn't have the wherewithal to dissect if this guy was exceptionally wild or if this was normal. I kind of just accepted things as they presented themselves. I left Arizona in the middle of my sophomore year and moved with family to North Dakota, and we stayed in touch by phone.

Paul did come visit me that summer and although no one knew it, he put a ring on my finger. Coming from dysfunctional backgrounds, neither of us had role models for marriage but that didn't matter. Beyond a doubt, that ring meant different things to each of us. I yearned for unconditional love, and the engagement was my immature "proof" that I had found it. We were young, dumb and in love. As best as we could understand it. Nothing stopped my thoughts from moving quickly between "marriage" and "family" and I fantasized about the children Paul and I would have together. Receiving unconditional love would be one thing, but pouring it out on children of my own would complete me! Even as a teenager, I knew that being a mother someday would fulfill me, give me purpose, and maybe even redeem some pieces of my own childhood that felt unfair. I had the heart of a mother, and I knew eventually I would have the experience. I only needed a little patience.

Paul was drafted in June of 1971. I was able to graduate early after getting approval from my mom and the superintendent of Mesa Public Schools. After all, I was engaged and was planning to follow my husband to North Carolina where he was stationed. We were married on November 8th, 1971. We had a "real" wedding and my brother-in-law gave me away. As soon as the semester was over, it was time to join my husband. I was naïve about so many things. I had never flown on a plane before, and I was anxious about switching planes in Texas. I was seated between two sweet old ladies who took me under their wings, which was comforting because this was not a smooth flight. I don't know all the details except, when we landed, they had foamed the runway which was lined with ambulances and police cars that were all awaiting our arrival. At one point during the commotion, I looked out the window and I saw the shadow of the plane and a rainbow in the distance, and it was one of those moments that I felt the peaceful presence of a God that I couldn't explain and didn't yet know. Paul picked me up from the airport and brought me to the mobile home that would become the place we would start our little family. I did not have to stay patient for long. I was pregnant within five months.

I should pause here and say, "What the heck were we thinking?" Time and wisdom and the vantage point I have now can see that those kids had no business starting a family. We had only ever known survival mode. I wasn't even convinced that Paul and I would make it. How do you expect to have a lifetime partner when you've never seen it work before? The dream was elusive but we were chasing it, sort of. We didn't have goals or plans beyond the immediate future and, in that moment, the only thing I cared much about was the baby growing inside of me. I was a child having a child and I had confidence that outsized my capabilities, but isn't that typical of young moms?

Eric Paul Edwards was born January 16th, 1973 in Fayetville,

North Carolina. He was 6 pounds, 11 ounces, 19 inches long. This blond haired, blue eyed baby was everything. He was perfection, and he was mine! How do I describe Eric? As a baby he was sickly. He couldn't tolerate formula; he cried and had horrible colic. He and I would walk tummy to tummy and we would both cry our eyes out. But I was on Cloud 9. This is what I was made for, and I didn't resent any of it for even a moment. I took him to the doctor at nine days old and looking back, I realize the medicine we were given smelled a lot like whisky, but it worked and we moved through that phase, eventually. We still had lots of doctor appointments, but between them, Eric was keeping us on our toes. He was a precocious boy, strong willed, smart, always pushing boundaries. He was my main source of entertainment and I took pictures of him every day. I was enamored. He was enamored. We were each other's world. A funny story comes to mind. When he was about 18 months old, he loved to eat Saltine Crackers. He would toddle over to me, I would give him a cracker, and he would disappear for a minute and come back for more. When I realized the box of crackers was emptying faster than a baby could consume it, I discovered that he had opened a kitchen drawer and was slipping his tiny arm behind it and saving crackers for later. He was mischievous and maybe slightly naughty and so curious. I loved him with my entire heart.

Paul and I were both so young, and we had much to learn, but he was a good support for me and Eric. I'm so grateful we didn't give up on each other, because we eventually got things right. Had we split when Eric was small, we would not have had each other when we lost him, and the only thing worse than going through a tragedy is going through one alone. Paul got out of the military in May of 1973. We quickly headed back to Mesa with our baby and our poodle in tow. We found an apartment, and we got civilian jobs. Paul was working for a cement company, and I was working as a unit secretary at the hospital. When it was time to have our second child, I was overjoyed at the thought and also terrified that I would never love another child the way I loved Eric. Did I have room in my heart for another? I'm convinced God multiplies a mother's love as many times as He needs to. It cannot be drained and it cannot be explained. It just is.

Jason Lee Edwards was born December 15th, 1977. He was opposite of his brother in every way imaginable. Despite my fears about it, my intense love for him was instant and I could hardly believe I had two boys. Two sons. Jason was the easiest baby. He rarely cried, he was healthy and loving. I actually felt guilty because he was content to stay in his carrier and required so little from me. I was constantly thinking, "Shouldn't we be at the doctor for something?" But he was just a dreamy baby, which was a great way to complete our family of four. Over the years we saw how different our two sons were. Jason always did look up to Eric, but he sized things up pretty quickly. While Eric was a bit chaotic, messy, and busy, Jason was orderly, tidy and controlled. It was fun watching their personalities unfold. People say this about kids, "If you have two, you have a variety," and I understood that. Our lives were rolling along, things were okay but they were about to change in a big way. We were about to find Jesus.

My only previous exposure to church was when I was about 12 years old. My dad had been on the construction team that built Trinity Baptist Church and although he wasn't personally interested, he signed us up for Vacation Bible School. During a missionary speech at VBS, there was an altar call. My 12 year old heart responded to that altar call, and I never forgot about it. I just didn't know what to do with it. The pastor there (Pastor Falconer) became important to me. He would eventually marry me and Paul. His son Tim owns the funeral home in Gilbert where we had Eric's body sent. It's a small world.

By this time in our story, it's 1980 and we are chugging along. I had gone to school and was working as a medical assistant. Paul was working in the auto body industry and we had purchased a home. We were introduced to friends of friends, and when they shared their life story, it resonated with us. We were looking for something. Paul was really looking for something. When we witnessed the dramatic transformation this couple had experienced and they invited us to church, we couldn't see why not. We went to church on a Sunday morning and by Monday night we had Baptists in our home for visitation. The following Sunday Paul responded to the altar call and we were full speed ahead. The Baptists do such a great job of shepherding new believers and we were insatiable for every bit of it. Week long revivals every night? Count us in. AWANA (Bible training) for the kids? Absolutely. We didn't miss a thing. The ever-present fear in me said, "This won't last. Everything ends. Don't get too emotionally involved." But we pursued. And if you know anything about churches, they split, people move along, each vein of Christianity is a little bit different. But we stayed in it. By 1986 we had been introduced to a mega-church in Mesa called Word of Grace. This Charismatic culture was unfamiliar, but we encountered a lot of counseling and healing there. This would be the church where our kids would attend youth group and where we would stay put through Eric's death and beyond.

We weren't perfect but we were doing it! I had my hubby and my boys and we were happy. I had a newfound love and identity in Jesus. I had personal goals to finish nursing school and begin my career. It was beginning to look like some things actually were "for keeps." I felt optimistic and excited, and although I didn't feel insulated from the troubles of this world, I felt like we were putting a stop to some of the generational chaos and pain that we had endured.

I blinked and when I opened my eyes, the kids were teenagers and my world was changing again. Raising teenage boys is not for the weak. I have heard neither is raising teenage girls, but I can only speak to my own experience. Teens show you what they want you to see, and they often tell you what you want to hear. Moms especially want what teenage boys are unwilling to give, in the form of more communication, more time, and more insight into their life. They need to spread their wings and assert some independence, and although our interest and questions come from a place of love, to them it feels like control. At some point, we have to trust what we taught them and the foundation we built, and let go a little. If we don't offer them any freedom, they will take it by force. Teens simply can't be monitored at all times.

"Teenage Eric" was small in stature but he had a big personality and always a few tricks up his sleeve. He had a spark in his eye and an inclination to "shenanigans" that were mostly innocent. To me, he was still that curious toddler, keeping me on my toes, keeping me guessing, sometimes driving me a little crazy. He had the same charming personality and ability to amuse me, he had simply grown a few feet taller! As an early teen, he spent a lot of time at our church's youth group, which was within our comfort zone. As it turns out the "church girls" found him intriguing, and he made friends and girlfriends at the camps, lock-ins, and all the other "Christian kid" activities that were offered. Within a church culture, a lot of your friends and acquaintances are by default. They are the people you spend your Sundays and Wednesdays with. I think there comes a point in every teen's life when they want to step out of the box their parents created, see who they connect with, and push the boundaries a bit. They want to see how other people live.

All that to say, friends are a big part of a teenager's life and to be honest there were times we doubted the kids' choices. But we welcomed their friends into our home and treated them with kindness. There was one kid, Josh, who came over several times and - spoiler alert- he would become a codefendant in my son's murder. Eric was no angel, and I'm not going to portray him as one, but he was probably in a little over his head with this new group of kids.

Another important milestone in a teenage boy's life is when he gets his first car. In Eric's case, it was a white 1982 Ford Escort. Because of Paul's line of work, he was always buying wrecked cars that he could fix up, and this one became a project for Eric and Paul to work on together. They shaved off the door handles, opened up part of the back for a huge speaker, and added some very fancy yellow and neon paint detailing to the exterior. They bonded over their project, and I'm so glad they had that experience together. Eric was proud of that car.

Just months before his death, Eric's friend group changed. He was dating a girl from Gilbert, her name was Shannon (not to be confused with my collaborative writer who is also a "Shannon"), and we really liked her. She was kind, smart and beautiful, a petite strawberry blonde. Understandably, Eric was smitten. Most importantly, it seemed like she had a good head on her shoulders and an established group of friends. Several times Eric brought this group of kids to church, and it seemed to us that he was maturing, choosing more carefully, and enjoying more wholesome company. Did I sense the calm before the storm? Not necessarily. Eric was dating a sweet girl, interested in church again, and working at the Taco Bell just up the road from our home. I was in nursing school. Paul was working for State Farm. Jason was in junior high school. Everyone was checking their boxes.

December 4th, 1991 was a regular day for the Edwards Family. The semester was nearing its end for me and I was counting down the days until break. I would still have one semester to finish my registered nurse degree, but the end was in sight. As I was driving home from school, I would pass Taco Bell and it would bring me a moment of peace to see that Eric's car was right there where it should be. Moms do this all the time. It's subconscious but it's repetitive. We run through the list of our family members to make sure we have tabs on everyone. Paul? At work. Check. Jason? At school. Check. Eric? At work. Wait. Where was Eric's car? I was uneasy for a half second and then thought, "Debbi. You've got his schedule wrong." Or, "Debbi. He must not be feeling well and he stayed home." Or, "Debbi. He's having car trouble". Those are the obvious reasons your child's car isn't where you expect it to be. "Debbi, don't be silly. Just because his car isn't there doesn't mean he isn't."

That evening revealed that Eric was in fact, not at work. He also wasn't at home or with Shannon. We had no answers. We lived in an upstairs apartment, and I watched Eric's parking spot from the window all night long. Someone did park in his regular spot for a while, which played cruel tricks on my mind, but it wasn't him. The next day I went to school as usual but when I got back he was still gone, so I called the Mesa Police Department. They weren't worried. My classmates at school didn't seem worried either. "This is what teenagers do; he'll show up; they always come back." I was advised to wait 72 hours to report a missing person, and although that's what the law says to do, this mom's biggest fear was becoming a reality. Eric was missing and I knew it.

2

Two Weeks

L OOKING BACK, THERE were some signs. The months leading up to Eric's disappearance were unusual. On one hand, there were some promising signs that he was maturing and looking forward to the future. As I mentioned, he was dating someone we really cared for, and I still believe they would have eventually married. He was easing back into church life and hanging out with a crowd we were much more comfortable with. We had the best ever Mother's Day celebration that May. Paul and I had gone to church in the morning, and the boys stayed back. We met them for lunch, and I was greeted with cards and flowers on the table. It was one of the first times the boys had honored me without Paul's guidance. We were proud of the boys, we knew this was a milestone that indicated our "babies" were growing up! Eric signed the card "USN" because he was seriously thinking about going into the Navy. It was one of those days that I looked at my little family and my heart overflowed with love and gratitude and anticipation of what the next few years might bring. I pictured Eric and Shannon following in mine and Paul's footsteps. A young bride and a few years in the military would be good for him. And I secretly dreamed of becoming a grand-mother someday.

But there were dark things happening as well. Strange occur-rences. Strange conversations. Looking back, I can see Eric's fear was escalating and we had no idea why he sometimes seemed uneasy or concerned. Again, teenagers have a lot going on inter-nally and weeding through "adolescent issues" versus "imminent danger" depends on their transparency with you. Eric never said he feared for his life, but he did tell me once that he never thought he would see his thirties. Obviously, this isn't something a parent wants to hear, but how do you respond when the thought of your child being murdered is the furthest thing from your mind? You remind them of how much you love them, God's plan for their life, and then you chalk it up to youthful drama. Once, someone threw a heavy object through Eric's bedroom window and one time a "Crazy Jesus Lady" called me to tell me that the enemy had set a trap for Eric, and if he didn't change his path, it would take his life. Again, how does a parent respond to such things? The lady was out of line. What did she know? Eric WAS changing his path. But his past was in hot pursuit, relentless to destroy him before he could overcome it.

December 4th was a Wednesday, and it was the day I drove past Taco Bell on my way home from school and noticed Eric's car wasn't there. Before I left for school at 7:30 that morning, I had gone into his bedroom to kiss his forehead, tell him I loved him, and leave the rent check with him. He would drop it off for me before heading to work. This was the night that I stood at my window - waiting, hoping and praying to see the white Escort with the bright graphics pull into "Eric's Spot". My heart knew something was terribly wrong, but I tried to stay hopeful and reasonable. Despite my son's sometimes wild ways, he wasn't really one to stay out all night or not communicate with us, and definitely not with Shannon. This first night, I resisted calling the police and letting my anxiety completely overtake me. I didn't know it at the time, but this was the day our family's nightmare began.

I did go to school on Thursday, not knowing it would be the last time that semester. I hesitantly shared my fears with fellow students and friends who joked with me that "teenagers always come back," and reassured me there was nothing to worry about. Once again, I drove past the Taco Bell on my way home, and once again, Eric's car was nowhere to be seen. I called Mesa Police Department and was told, "He's an adult, and a missing person's report cannot be filed for 72 hours." So, without any police help, we drove around looking, searching all of Eric's usual hangouts. Shannon's neighborhood. Her best friend Jennifer's neighborhood. The area around Red Mountain High School and local parks. Paul and his brother Roy printed flyers with pictures of Eric and his car and posted them in business windows all over Mesa. Our searching would be fruitless, but we were hopeful that once the police were involved, they could cast a wider net and figure out what was going on.

After a day or two, our home phone was starting to ring. It was 1991 and we did not have cell phones, of course. We lived in a world of pagers, answering machines, and call backs. I did not have school on Fridays so I kept Jason by my side, and we sat by the phone interviewing every single person who rang. Paul and his brother Roy spent the day beating the streets and searching as we had the night before. A strange thing happens when a teen disappears. First of all, some people are attracted to drama. But as everyone knows, teens love it, and we were dependent on teens for information that would lead us to Eric. Sorting through the information that was coming our way was like looking for a diamond in the rough. Over the next 12 days there would be rumors of gangs, drugs, senseless feuds, and jealousy. There were a few names and a group of kids that popped up repeatedly. One girl, Michelle, called constantly to report what her boyfriend Marcus was saying about the case. At one point, she mentioned a beef over stolen audio equipment and gave me a couple of specific names. I don't believe she was trying to throw the case off, because what she provided was useful. I do think she enjoyed the attention. Her boyfriend, Marcus, was interviewed and eventually cleared. I think he knew exactly what had happened and was being braggadocious about it. I guess they both liked the attention that came from being "in the know" when heinous crimes were being committed. She said to me once, "They lived to terrorize him." And when I looked back over the past few months, I could see that when Eric was displaying signs of concern or anxiety, he was probably sparing me from the full effects of the terror he was living in.

By Saturday, it had been 72 hours and I was counting the minutes until I could file a Missing Persons' Report. When I finally got through to a Detective Bowser, she refused to take it. She said, "Your son is not a juvenile. He is not disabled. He is not endangered, and he wasn't taken involuntarily." She then went on to say, "You know these kids. They are like a pack of dogs. They just run off and do their own thing. They will do things in a group they would never do on their own. He's fine, he's just emboldened by the crowd." I'm not normally one to challenge authority or assert myself but I piped up loudly, "HOW DO YOU KNOW?" Silently screaming, "Are you a mom? What if this were your kid? Please help us!" I could not understand why she would not show any compassion or have any belief in my intuition as a mom or as a woman. Her response was heartless.

So, I kept calling. All day long. Every thought I had, I called and reported. I gave them the VIN number of the car, told them all the identifying things I could about the vehicle and Eric, and shared what I had learned so far. I just wanted things on record, official or unofficial, I didn't care. I exasperated the police (and they did finally take the Missing Persons' Report). Saturday evening,

Paul and I went to church. At the end of the service, the pastor invited people in need of prayer to come forward. He looked over to me and Paul, and raised his eyebrows, a silent invitation to make ourselves available to people in need. It was after we prayed for other families and their situations that we shared with our pastor what we were going through. His statement will stay with me forever, "We just don't always know the weight people are carrying." Isn't that the truth?

On Sunday, December 8th, we made a stolen vehicle report. We couldn't get any attention that our son, a human being infinitely more precious than a vehicle, was gone, so we concluded maybe they would pursue this from another angle. Finally, Mesa Police Department came out and met with us in person. Detective Pomush. It's been hard to forgive Detective Pomush. He was condescending, belittling and absolutely cruel to us. At one point, he shoved pictures of the car and of Eric at us and said, "This is your son, and this is his car. We know more about him than you do. You need to back off." That was a dark moment. But later that day Shannon and a few of Eric's other friends came over for a visit. They brought a live Christmas tree with them and proceeded to decorate the tree and our apartment for Christmas. It was such a kindness. I loved those kids, they were good kids.

Here's a bit of a tangent. We have always been pro-police and law abiding citizens. We are grateful for the work they do to keep our community safe, absolutely. However, Mesa Police Department was not pleasant to work with. They treated our family in crisis as an inconvenience and insinuated that our "wayward teen" was causing our agony and that he would return like a prodigal when he was ready. I was doing my own detective work, a parallel investigation to the police, because they weren't keeping me in the loop. My phone was still ringing off the hook, and I was continually gathering information in my notebook that stayed next to the phone. Paul was trying to work, and Jason was going to school again, but I was fielding calls and doing my best to "chew the meat, spit out the bones" and relay anything relevant to MPD. It felt like an uphill battle and that was disheartening and unnecessary.

We received information that someone had seen Eric's car at the 7/11 on Ray and Alma School Road in Chandler on December 9th. Technology in 1991 was primitive compared to what we have now, but the VCR tape was retrieved and when I saw the grainy images I knew it wasn't Eric on the video. Moms know their children's mannerisms and their gait, and we can identify them from afar. I was so hopeful to see my son on that footage, for reassurance that he was still alive and still local, but it simply wasn't him, and we had to move on.

That same day, Paul received a phone call that Eric's car was found on fire in Whittier, California, about 40 minutes outside of Los Angeles. The police said it was a very hot fire, but there was enough proof remaining that when they cross referenced the missing person's database to the remnants of the vehicle, they could connect us. This was ominous news and the police began to take this case seriously because of it. However, a car is just a car, and the car did not have a body in it. Paul, Jason, and I went to the police station that day to confirm that the car was indeed ours and verify the next step; we would continue searching for Eric and we would not stop until we found him.

By December 12th, the family had provided Mesa Police with Eric's dental and medical records. The thought was, hopefully, these will never be needed, but…just in case. What would I do if I found out Eric was dead? Simple. I would die too. Maybe not a physical death, but certainly an emotional one. My very purpose in life would be questioned. I was made to be Eric's mother, and without him, a part of me would simply die with him. I pushed that thought down, and down, and down and busied myself collecting leads and conducting interviews. Shannon's best friend Jennifer was interviewed the same day, and she brought up the same few names that had been circulating. She told the police that she didn't suspect foul play but it was likely that Eric needed to get away from these boys. We, on the other hand were distraught that Eric had been gone a full week. The discovery of his burnt car led us to believe things were escalating. It was in the air, we could feel it.

The next week was mostly more of the same. Phone calls. Racing minds. Trying to handle the "normal" work and school responsibilities. I ended up missing the last week of school and two big finals. I was staying in communication with my teachers, crossing every "T" and dotting every "I" because even then I was determined to finish school. Paul was still searching the streets at night, and his brother had lit up the marquis at their auto body shop with bright letters "ERIC CALL HOME". Little contact came from Mesa Police (although in hind sight and in looking through transcripts of interviews that were recorded at all hours of the night – I need to give a little credit where it's due. The police were working the case more than I believed at the time). We were on our knees praying, hoping, watching, and wishing our son would walk through the door. It wouldn't matter what his story was or if he told us anything at all. We desperately wanted him home and to put this hellish week behind us. As a family, we could handle whatever had caused this nightmare. As soon as our son was home, we would work together to get back on track, heal from this trauma, and get to work on the next steps for each of us.

I need to mention December 15th. Besides the continuing and steady stream of misinformation and rumors that were swirling, this was Jason's 14th birthday. So many times over the years I have experienced "mom guilt" about that day. So many times I have apologized to Jason that we were too distracted to celebrate him. So many times Jason has reassured me that he understood and he understands. Jason did receive a special gift that day, a Cockatiel from his uncle. On one hand, the last thing our family needed was another responsibility. On the other hand, God's creatures can provide such a pure distraction when life, as you know it, is coming apart, and Jason deserved that.

December 17th was a big day. First, two news reporters came and interviewed us at home. The interview was aired here in Arizona, and it was also shared to NBC in Los Angeles. Mesa Police Department had put up a $500 reward for information, presumably because teenagers likely had answers and that sum would be enough to tempt them to talk. The second noteworthy mention was a meeting we had with a different Mesa Police Officer. We had grown up with Officer Poulin and although he wasn't assigned to this case, he invited us to meet him at his station. He told me, "Debbi, we have officers in Los Angeles right now; this is being investigated as a homicide." He did not reveal any specific details besides that. When we walked outside, I leaned against a tree and absolutely fell apart. The sound of a mother's sobs when she loses a child is unlike anything in the world. It is guttural, primal and unhinged because a piece of us is ripped away and the pain can't be described with human words. I knew, I had known for days, but he confirmed. Sometimes we choose denial, but moms know. I knew when Eric's tummy was hurting as an infant. I knew he was being a sneaky toddler and hiding his snacks. I knew he had chosen the wrong crowd of friends, and I knew his life was in danger when he went missing. This was the day I had to acknowledge it.

The next day, our world truly shattered. We had been simultaneously waiting for and dreading this news for two weeks. December 18th, 1991 we learned the truth about the events leading up to and including our son's brutal murder and aftermath. December 18th marked the beginning of a 27 year journey for me, the wildest ride a heart can take. Here is the revelation of the true events surrounding my son's death:

Eric had been running with a crowd of rough kids. None of them had anything of their own; they had been bounced from home to home, kicked out of school, experimented with drugs and alcohol and looked up to gangsters. As we know, angry young men always have something to prove, and these kids were looking for validation in all the wrong places. Eric was trying to sever ties with them, but he worked and lived in close proximity and he had one thing they didn't – transportation – and via intimidation and familiarity, Eric still provided them rides when they asked.

Josh was a 17 year old kid I mentioned earlier. He had been to our house several times and we liked him well enough. I actually didn't realize "our Josh" was this Josh until his first hearing, because the police had been using his formal name, Joshua, and I hadn't connected those dots. That was sad. The second name that came up a lot was "Pete" (which is not his legal name, but it is his "street name" that I will use throughout this book). He was a 20 year old guy who was living with Josh at the time, and who worked at the Peter Piper Pizza that was in the same parking lot as "Eric's" Taco Bell. Pete was older than the rest of the group, and he was a big dude. Intimidating. He called himself "The Mayor" because he kind of ran things. He had influence over these younger, smaller teens and he used it. Josh's criminal behaviors and poor choices escalated when Pete came into the picture. The third name that continued popping up was Marcus. Supposedly Eric and Marcus were having some issues over car speakers. I may never know the truth about those speakers, but I have seen the receipt for them - $121. I would have given every one of those kids $121 if it would have spared my son's life, but ultimately I don't think the speakers were as important to this story as we were initially led to believe.

On December 1st, Josh stole a couple of guns from another acquaintance's home. It was pre-arranged, and that was a separate crime of its own. Josh and Pete each kept a gun, presumably to be used for robberies. Or maybe just to fulfill their own fantasies and increase their "street cred". In any event, Josh claimed his plan was to use the gun for a robbery on the morning of December 4th. In a later statement, according to Josh, Pete said that morning, "I'm going to kill Eric Edwards today." So, they asked Eric to come pick them up that morning. Did Eric know of their nefarious plans? Did Josh believe Pete? I can't answer. I suppose anything is possible. I would like to believe that if Eric did know about Josh's plan, he went along only because of fear, coercion, or threats.

As the story goes, the three boys drove around for a while that morning of December 4th. Eric was in the driver's seat. Josh was in the passenger seat. Pete was sitting behind Eric. It was 9:30 am. The boys were driving east on McKellips and had just passed Power Road when a completely unprovoked Pete shot Eric through the back of his seat. He then proceeded to reach around the seat and shoot Eric five more times before steering the car onto the shoulder of the road. Understandably, Josh was in shock and scared, so he agreed to help dispose of the body in a nearby desert wash. Have you been to the Arizona desert? Even just a few feet off of a well-traveled road, it is desolate. Shades of brown and tan mostly, with less-than-vibrant pops of color, except the quick blooms we enjoy in early spring. Natives will tell you about the desert in bloom, "Blink and you miss it", and we mean that. Creosote bushes. Saguaro. Cholla. They have a beauty all their own but they are not a vibrant green. The earth is often cracked from the last rain, which could have been many moons before. When the desert gets a storm, the earth is often so hard that it can't soak the rain up fast enough so flooding occurs, and it creates deep grooves and cracks in the desert floor. The Superstition Mountains are a beautiful back drop to the suburbs just east of Phoenix, and they have hiking trails throughout. But, when you are off-trail in the open desert, what you will find is harsh and inhabitable for humans. It IS however, a great place to dump a body, considering people don't wander around much for fear of dehydration, rattle snakes, and scorpions. Before covering his body with limbs and debris, Pete reached into Eric's pocket and pulled out about $60. They did rob someone that day. My son. 7600 E. McKellips Road was the address given for my son's murder. Near his body the police would find a few articles of clothing, a bloody towel, and a Taco Bell apron. Eventually, someone (I never did find out who) put a cross up in the area, and it stayed there for a long time.

Josh and Pete took Eric's car and stayed at a "no tell motel" on Main Street that night. They drank beer and went to the mall and presumably tried to get their stories straight. By 4:00 am on December 5th, Pete was back at Josh's home and Josh was on the road to California in Eric's car. He was headed to the Los Angeles area where his father lived. He had taken with him one of the stolen guns, three bags of clothes, and 50 cents. He would panhandle for gas to make the trip.

This next part of the tale gets a little confusing. Luckily, following these twist-and-turn details will not impact your understanding of the outcome…

Over the next few days Pete and Josh were speaking regularly. And so were the police in Los Angeles with the police in Mesa. Per Pete's advice, Josh had set the car on fire in California and, as I mentioned before, the police cross-referenced the VIN to missing persons' reports. The process that would culminate on December 18th began escalating on the 9th with the discovery of the car. Josh's family here in Arizona was cooperative when the police came knocking. Pete came across as cooperative as well and initially he was pretty convincing. He placed the blame on Marcus, essentially replacing himself in the story with Marcus. There were a couple of awkward recorded phone calls between Josh and Pete in which Pete was deflecting and speaking in code, trying to make sure he and Josh would keep a straight story, but it was unraveling. Josh was unwilling to send Marcus away for something Pete did, and, he was ready to tell the truth.

Josh's mom encouraged him to do the right thing and come back to Arizona. Simultaneously, police had a search warrant, plus permission from Josh's mother to search her home, and they recovered Pete's gun from the room he and Josh were sharing. It was convoluted because Pete continued interviewing and continued trying to put Marcus in it, but the police were steadily poking holes in that story. Pete didn't know it yet, the details were still fuzzy, but Josh had already caved.

Josh flew back to Arizona, and was met at Sky Harbor by his mother and two officers. He led police straight into the desert and to Eric's body. While the area was secured for an investigation, Josh and his mom were taken to interrogation, and he told the whole truth, confirming Pete was the shooter and Marcus was innocent. Josh never went home that day. His list of six charges includes burglary, arson, aggravated assault and hindering a prosecution. He was remanded into the adult system. He gave Pete up that day and was able to plea down his charges because of it.

Pete was also arrested on the 18th of December. He maintained his innocence all the way to the end and he thought he could outsmart the police, but ultimately, the police had Josh's story as well as Pete's shoe prints from the scene, and the smoking gun from his room. Pete alone would be charged with Eric's murder.

The night of December 18th, the police and our dear friends from church, Larry and Lynn, came to update us on the case and the arrests. I can't say I was surprised when I learned who was involved. All of the calls I had taken and all of the rumors I had heard weren't too far from the truth. Paul, Jason and I stayed the night with Larry and Lynn. They were a great comfort and we trusted them to help us get through the next devastating task. Our heads were spinning, our hearts were broken, the future was uncertain, and our family was forever changed. And we now had a funeral to plan.

Discussion Questions
Part 1

1. Do you believe some hurt is so profound it can never be fully healed or forgiven?

2. How do "young Debbi's" thoughts on being a wife differ from her thoughts on being a mother? Why? Do you relate?

3. When Debbi and Paul became Christians, many aspects of their family life changed for good, but tragedy still struck their family. What are your thoughts on a Christian's response to tragedy? How does a trial of this magnitude affect our faith and our ability to believe in God's goodness toward us?

4. How does parenting teens today differ from 1991? Has improved technology and the availability of tracking devices changed the behavior of teenagers? Their parents? Law enforcement?

5. How do you suspect Eric's murder will change the course of Debbi, Paul and Jason's lives? What coping mechanisms do we turn to in desperation?

PART TWO:

Hate

3

Saying Goodbye

THE FUNERAL WAS set for December 21st, just three short days after Eric was found. We didn't choose that day. Just like so many other things, it was chosen for us by a church community, family and friends who swept in and loved us in the most practical and selfless ways anyone could hope for. Although Paul and I were walking around in a blur, things were being done on our behalf to honor Eric that we never could have put together. Although so many of those people have lost touch or gone home to Heaven themselves, we are still so grateful for them. I won't remember everything, and the things that I do recall may not be what you would expect, but here is my recollection of the few days between December 18th and 21st, 1991.

My first prayer upon hearing Eric was gone, was to ask the Lord to help me remember the details, remember the feelings, remember…him. I felt a responsibility to carefully steward Eric's legacy. For some victims that looks like advocating for reform or creating non-profits or being a loud voice in the community. For me, it meant navigating the grief process appropriately, with dignity, and not allowing myself to "get stuck". It never occurred to me that I would share this story in a book, but I'm grateful that

34 years later I am able to recall the details and feelings I prayed would stay with me.

Did we sleep the night of the 18th? I don't recall. Most nights we tossed and turned, slept in shifts, or just resigned ourselves to sleeplessness. We knew we would get up the next morning and spend the day making decisions that no parent should ever have to make. What color casket did I want for my son? Well, let me think. I didn't want a casket for my son. Blue. The 19th was a day full of decisions we never wanted to make, places we didn't want to be, conversations we never wanted to have, and trying our best to navigate how we would honor this life that was cut far too short.

When we got up that morning, it was raining. If you live in Arizona, you know this is not typical. I mean, it's not that it never rains, but it somehow always catches us by surprise and feels significant. Lynn said to me, "Debbi, even God is grieving today, He's crying". Nevertheless, there was no time to stay inside or wait it out. We had a list of places to go, and we would start by going to Falconer's Funeral Home.

We did choose a blue casket out of a large showroom of caskets. I remember it had silver handles and I chose a casket spray with red and black flowers, but beyond that I don't remember a lot of details. Eric's body was impossible to embalm because it was badly decomposed. Between the weather, animals, passage of time and maggots we knew there would be a closed casket graveside service for the family only. We still had to decide what to dress him in, and we chose some overall shorts and a t-shirt. This was his 18 year old "uniform" that he wore often, a reminder that he was too young to be in that box. Shannon had given him some Oakley sunglasses, and she wanted those in the casket with him. We were happy to oblige.

From the funeral home, the next stop is the cemetery. In our case we chose Mountain View Cemetery in East Mesa. How do you pick a plot for your son? It was narrowed down by a couple of factors; the baby plots were nearby as well as the plots of a couple military men. He was our baby and he had military goals so it seemed fitting I suppose. I remember the different sections of the cemetery had different names, but I don't recall the name of the area any longer. At the time this cemetery did not install headstones, only bronze grave markers. You select "options" from a list of upgrades and the price ticks up with every attachment you choose. The funeral industry is a business, and although they operate with sympathy and tact, I was startled by the cost each step of the way. This is definitely not something parents prepare for. We did have a permanent vase installed on Eric's marker and it's nice to see flowers in it when we stop by. The cemetery also handled the obituary for the newspaper, and they interviewed us for the press release.

There were two things that really bothered me. I was told that sometimes the graves are dug twice as deep and two people are buried in the same plot. That was just a no for me. I had to confirm this wouldn't happen. I had to be absolutely certain. The second thing was the text on the grave marker. I really wanted Eric's exact birth date and exact date of death listed. Maybe because his life was so short it felt like every single day should be counted. This is a real person who was born on a specific date and was gone on a specific date. It may not mean much to anyone else but to me it was important. I was sad to simply see 1973-1991.

From the cemetery we went to the church to make the program for the memorial service. Larry's secretary typed it up for us and we had it printed at Kinko's. My mom's favorite poem was "Footprints in the Sand" which was fitting, so we had that printed on the inside left of the program. I chose a couple of songs and somehow arrangements were made for musicians to play and sing the selections. This all came together very quickly, and once again, people were stepping in to handle details that we had neither the time nor energy to do on our own. December 19th was an absolute whirlwind, but we got everything we needed to achieve for the service handled. On the 20th all I needed to do was shop for an outfit in preparation for what would be one of the toughest days of my life.

One night I dreamed I was walking along the beach with the Lord.
Many scenes from my life flashed across the sky.
In each scene I noticed footprints in the sand.
Sometimes there were two sets of footprints,
Other times there were one set of footprints.
This bothered me because I noticed
That during the low periods of my life,
When I was suffering from
Anguish, sorrow or defeat,
I could see only one set of footprints.
So I said to the Lord,
"You promised me Lord,
That if I followed you,
You would walk with me always.
But I have noticed that during the most trying periods of my life
There have only been one set of footprints in the sand.
Why, when I needed you most, have you not been there for me?"
The Lord replied,
"The times when you have seen only one set of footprints in the sand,
is when I carried you."
Author Unknown

We held the graveside service on the morning of the 21st, prior to the memorial service at Word of Grace. There were about 30 people in attendance, family and the closest friends. It's surreal when you see a hearse and a casket with your baby in it. So many times I asked myself, "How can this be real?" and, "Is this real?" But every time I tried to snap out of it I was confronted with the painful truth; I was here, at my eldest son's funeral, and the service was beginning. Two of our pastor friends spoke, and I know they made it meaningful. I wish I could remember it perfectly. Here's what I do remember. I remember learning that people are always buried facing East so they can watch for Christ's return. I remember people laying long-stemmed roses on top of the casket. My sister Christy had passed them out to everyone at the service. I remember walking up and putting my hands on the casket and struggling badly with the idea of leaving it, knowing it would be lowered into the ground and out of my sight forever. I remember my mind playing tricks on me over the finality of everything that was happening that day and what this service symbolized. I was going through the motions, mostly in a fog, with moments of lucidity. My life would be segmented like this for years to come. I would learn how to manage our day-to-day lives but in the background I was distracted by the weight of our tragedy.

When we went to the church for the memorial service, there were even more surprises. The news people were there, looking for an interview. I gave it to them and we have it on an old VHS tape somewhere. I wasn't offended by their presence or their request. They had followed the case and I was glad to do it. The detectives were there, in plain clothes of course. They were hoping to get more clues regarding the case. There were big, beautiful oversized collages with photos of Eric and tons of flowers, huge wreaths. I don't know who put most of this together. I know my nursing class was there with a wreath and banner that said "Code Blue 92" which was the name we gave ourselves when we started the program together.

We had 200 programs printed and we ran out long before people stopped coming through the doors. In true "Eric Fashion" the crowd was diverse. Almost comically diverse, looking back. We had church kids, gangster kids, preppy Gilbert High School kids, and some biker guys who found Paul in the lobby and reassured him that they would have Eric's killer "handled in prison". We didn't know who they were and we certainly didn't want anyone exacting revenge on our behalf so Paul politely declined their offer.

Shannon and Eric's song "(Everything I Do) I Do It For You" by Bryan Adams was looping as people walked into the sanctuary. Our lead pastor Gary Kinnaman spoke and once again so did our dear friend Larry. The one line I remember from Gary's speech was, "We always ask questions. Why does a young kid have to die? And why like this?" It was such a tactful way to address a truth that was so abhorrent. It said so much with so few words. Gary ended the service with the salvation message. So many of the kids in Eric's life needed to hear about God's unconditional love for them. I pray many seeds were planted that day and some of these young people will join us in Heaven.

The first song we selected was "Home Free" by Wayne Watson. Greg and Karla, our worship leaders at church sang and our friend Barbara accompanied. Maybe there were dry eyes in the room, but with lyrics that perfectly described our grappling with the kindness of God, while being simultaneously leveled with grief, probably meant there weren't many.

The second song was performed by a friend from our Baptist church that we were attending before Word of Grace. I always thought Elaine's voice was beautiful and she was the perfect choice to sing "We Shall Behold Him" by Sandi Patti.

Beyond the beautiful music and messages from our pastors, our niece Sheila shared an original poem, and our niece Sharlene read some of Jason's favorite memories with his brother on his behalf. Poor Jason. My heart still aches when I think about certain pieces of his life. Paul wanted to speak at the service, which is something that our pastor had never seen before. But, it was important to him to share, and he did an amazing job. We can only chalk it up to supernatural strength for that moment and a father's message that needed telling.

Following the service there was a "receiving line" for people to walk through and offer their condolences. There were unexpected people in the crowd. A few faces stood out to me, and when I wondered how they knew, I realized they had been following this story on the news. Dr. Packer, Eric's pediatrician was there. Many of my friends from class attended and even some professors. When one of my professors, Mrs. Brooks came through, she leaned over and whispered to me, "Debbi. You've got an A in my class and so much more." It turns out my sister Cathy had typed my term paper and submitted it on my behalf. This was another example of our community stepping in for us, knowing what we needed and serving us with such pure hearts, asking for nothing in return.

Since we weren't expecting such a massive crowd at the memorial, we had planned a luncheon at my mom's house for after the service. When we asked the pastor to announce that "all were welcome to join us" he wanted to clarify…all? Many people did come over and it was a nice open house style gathering. The collages and flowers were brought from the church and displayed. There were friends there I hadn't seen in a long time, even a friend from North Dakota, but I was going through the motions and couldn't easily connect with people. I didn't eat a thing. I remember we saved a few flowers to be preserved, and that when the last friend left, we were physically and emotionally spent.

We went back to our apartment the evening of the 21st. We had been given a leather pouch that was filled with keepsakes from the day and sympathy cards. We flopped onto our couch and began looking through the pouch and the guest book. We wouldn't make it through everything in one sitting. There was just so much. Many of the cards had money in them, which was kind. I didn't realize people put money in sympathy cards until then but now I always do the same. There are unexpected expenses and missed work and fast food runs when you are going through this process. We appreciated the generosity. One of the cards had a very personal letter enclosed. At the time I read the first few sentences and quickly folded it up and stuffed it away. I'll be sharing more about the letter soon, but it was dated December 18th, 1991 at 9:30 am…about six hours before Josh would lead police to Eric's body.

Finally, Paul and I looked at each other like, "What now? What do we do? Just go to bed?" And that's what we attempted to do. Between the anxiety and the agony, I was able to sleep off and on. Paul was struggling more than I was to rest. Sleeping soothed a bit of that day's pain, and I was thankful for it, but the road ahead of us would be longer and more complicated than we could have ever imagined. We would still need to endure a trial and everything that led up to it and came after it. I'll share about the trial later. I want to share the many miracles that occurred during these early years. There was no way to prepare my heart for this process, but God faithfully reminded us that He was there, and He gave us the strength to keep going, which sometimes felt like a miracle as well.

4

Little Miracles

EVERY TIME WE felt desperate, each time we thought we had reached the limits of our ability to cope with Eric's death, the Lord refilled us. He knows exactly what we need and when we need it and He is endlessly faithful to us. Each of these "little miracles" happened early in the journey, all of them happened before the trial started. They assisted in our recovery, and they prepared us for the harshness of the trial. There were still surprises in the trial, but knowing exactly how Eric died and where he was made it bearable and we were stronger than we suspected we would be. To this day, these stories give me goose bumps when I share them. The God of Miracles is always on the move.

Paul had a couple of meaningful experiences that he's shared over the years. Most of this book is "my" recollection, but I would like to share pieces of Paul's journey on his behalf. There are a couple impactful, important stories that prove the Lord was walking with him and encouraging his heart as He was also encouraging mine. A mother's heart and a father's heart are so different! The amazing thing is that our Lord understands them both perfectly. These are Paul's experiences, as I understand them:

Paul and Jason had gone to a father/son outing with our church. They were camping at Roosevelt Lake with a group of guys. Paul says they were sharing their life stories with each other, when a man confided that his son had committed suicide. Paul was just the right person to offer comfort and pray with him and he wells up with tears when he describes praying that the man would "see his son's face." In Heaven. Perfect. Restored. Healthy and whole.

Paul's long commute to work took him through parts of an Indian reservation that were pretty desolate, quiet and long. One morning he was praying, yelling at God for letting Eric die. He shares that the Lord spoke to his heart, "I know how you feel, my son died too." Taken aback, Paul yelled out in frustration, "But you got to raise your son!" and he felt the Lord speak to his heart once again, "And I raised your son too." This "exchange" was immediately followed with an image. Sometimes the Lord is so gracious to give us pictures in our minds of the things we need to see or allow us to "hear" the things that will realign us to His truth. Paul explains he "saw" Eric in Heaven. Eric and Pete in Heaven. Eric with his arm around Pete's waist in a "guy side hug." And the next thing he heard in his heart was Eric's voice saying, "It's cool, Dad." That comforted him greatly and he shares that story to this day.

The next few miracles are "mine". I always call them "My Five Little Miracles". They overlapped with Paul's experiences but these were personal, straight from the Lord, designed to comfort me.

The Lord is close to the brokenhearted and saves those who are crushed in spirit. Psalm 34:18 NIV

Miracle 1. December, 1991. The day we were running around making funeral preparations, I was dead on my feet. Larry's secretary was typing up the bulletin and Lynn said, "Debbi, why don't you go into the sanctuary and lie down for a bit? We will let you know when we need you." I walked into the big, empty sanctuary that was decorated beautifully for Christmas. I could feel the peace of God as I absorbed the silence, looking at the cross that was always front and center on the stage, and marveling at the beauty of it all. As I was drifting off to sleep in the pew, I was praying, and my prayer was, "Lord. I need connection. I need to connect with another mom whose child was murdered. I need to know that someone understands." The Lord answered my heart instantly, "Mary knows how you feel. Her son was murdered too." It's not something we think about often, that Jesus had a mother who raised Him, loved Him, and despite knowing He was Messiah, grieved her loss when He was taken from her. Here I was, surrounded by evidence of His birth (the Christmas decorations) and evidence of His death (the cross) and it hit me hard that Jesus as deity was called to die, but as a human being He was simply murdered.

Miracle 2. May, 1992. The night of the funeral as Paul and I were opening cards, one card had a long letter fall out of it. It was dated 9:30 am on December 18th and Eric's body was found around 3:30 pm that same day. I began to read the letter and quickly disregarded it. The lady who wrote it (Lana) said that while she was praying she saw a vision of Eric in the back of a fast moving vehicle. He was shot, he was scared, and he knew he was dying. I was done right there. I had been told that Eric was in the driver's seat and died immediately with one fatal shot. He didn't know what hit him. I folded that letter up, shoved it back in the leather pouch and hardened my heart to the validity of it. Period. The following May, after school was out for me, I found myself having a really hard day and extra time on my hands. I was home alone, the house was quiet, and I was drawn to that pouch again. By this time, I had learned the truth…Eric had been shot multiple times, he even had defensive wounds, and he was transferred to the hatchback of his car while he was still alive. He indeed would have been scared and most likely aware that his life was ending, as the car sped into the desert on that horrible day. I hated the thought of it with every ounce of my soul, but knowing that the beginning of the letter had actually been accurate, I kept reading. The next part of the letter said that Jesus himself escorted Eric to Heaven. That was like a hug from the Lord. If the first part of Lana's vision was so perfectly accurate, why should I doubt the second part? I found Lana at church the following Sunday and thanked her for the gift she gave me. It took five months to read that letter in its entirety, but when I did, it was in the Lord's timing, and it was another step towards eventual peace.

Miracle 3. May, 1992. I found myself in the exact same church sanctuary I had been so many times on Mother's Day throughout the years, this time with one less child to celebrate me. This is the same place I had been lying on the pew before Eric's funeral and felt the Lord telling me that Mary understood me. Just as Mary had "pondered things in her heart," I had been doing the same. I was not running around telling people, "The Lord told me I have a special connection to Mary, the Mother of God." I doubted everything, and also that sounds a bit strange, so I kept it to myself. There was always time during the service to "greet your neighbor" and that day there were many "Happy Mother's Day!" greetings in the mix. Imagine my surprise when an acquaintance sitting behind me pulled me close and whispered, "Happy Mother's Day, Debbi. God knows you are identifying with Mary right now. He has given you this!" She had no idea what a gift that was. I had experienced two Mother's Days in a row that were precious. One in which my boys honored me with cards and flowers and a wonderful lunch together. The second was when God led a fellow believer to validate the very words He had spoken to me so clearly in December.

Miracle 4. October, 1992. Every fall there was a women's retreat at church. We would escape up to the cool mountains of Northern Arizona and spend a weekend in worship, teaching, prayer and fellowship. I was usually involved in the event planning and making sure all the attendees had a fantastic weekend, but this time it was my turn to receive. I went to that retreat with one question in mind, and I was anticipating confirmation of what that letter had said; Eric was with Jesus. There was a session that weekend that was intended to be quiet, deep and soul-searching. The friend I attended with knew I was seeking an encounter with the Lord and I told her, "I'm going to be praying for a while. Don't touch me or talk to me. I just need to be alone with the Lord." While I was praying, I saw the most beautiful vision. I knew I was looking at a Heavenly scene. There was a giant pyramid of white stairs in the dream. At the top of the stairs sat God the Father and next to him, Jesus was standing up. Eric was ascending the stairs toward them. I knew he was headed for an embrace. I was longing to see them hug - I was waiting for it - and someone touched me gently to get my attention. I lost it. I lost the moment. I was taken back to that conference room and real life in an instant. I wasn't angry about it, but I was disappointed. I headed home and I did feel grateful for that experience, but I felt it was half-finished. The next week, our niece called and asked if she could bring us something. She was an amateur artist and wanted to give us a painting that she had been working on. It was a painting of Eric and Jesus and they were hugging! This was another time that the Lord used someone else to bless me, to finish what was started, and to confirm in this mom's heart that we were being sustained by our loving creator. That painting has always hung right over my bed, and it always will.

Miracle 5. July, 1993. Despite all of this, I still needed closure. Closure is evasive when you lose someone this way and it's a process. One of our friends in the Marriage Accountability Group asked if seeing what remained of Eric's car would help, and I thought maybe it would. As far as I knew, the car was still in

California, and I was willing to fly there if needed. When I called to make arrangements with the police, I was met with another little miracle. Apparently, there was a trailer sent to California to pick up a vehicle that was police evidence in a separate crime, and while it was there they brought Eric's car back with it. So our car was sitting at a police impound lot in Mesa. It was easy to schedule an appointment to meet someone there, and they brought me straight to the car, which was burned beyond recognition. Almost. Just behind the rear tire on the driver's side, there was a section of the car that was still intact. It was not very big, maybe a foot long at most, but it was a perfectly preserved section of the graphic that was a one-of-a-kind custom and so easy to identify. I reached out and touched that paint and ran my hand over it. This was the last place my son was and that connection did in fact take me one step closer to closure. Seeing the car had served its purpose.

Nothing could bring Eric back, but the God of all comfort comes through. He meets us in our circumstances and He uses other people to bless us, so we may in turn bless others. There are times we "see in part" what He is doing, and we wish we could walk a little more by sight and a little less by faith. In my experience, He's weaving our story together with perfect timing and revealing details when our hearts need them most. The Bible says "in this world we will have trouble" and I knew that all too well. The second part of the verse says "but I give you my peace" and that was just as true. Total peace was still a long way off for me, but I was getting glimpses, and they kept me hanging on.

"I have told you these things, so that in me you may have peace. In this world you will have trouble. But take heart! I have overcome the world." John 16:33 NIV

$$5$$

The Hearings

LIFE GOES ON. Somewhat. Over the next several years we would pick up the pieces of our shattered hearts and try to figure out how to do life as a family of three.

Immediately after the funeral, Christmas was upon us. On Christmas Eve we were with Paul's side of the family. There was a lot of tip-toeing around the "elephant in the room" which we knew was an effort of compassion on their part. When you experience a loss like this you have to surround yourself by an enormous cloud of grace for others. They can't be responsible for knowing when you want to talk about your loved one, when you can't bear it, when your emotions are spinning out. Most people will avoid the topic as if they don't want to remind you of your pain, when the reality is that your pain is ever present anyway. I made a cassette tape of the funeral music as well as a song our friend Wade wrote and sang, and I gave copies to everyone. On Christmas Day we celebrated with my side of the family. There were lots of little kids running around and that was a good distraction. We were able to have a nice day.

Before we knew it, it was January of 1992. Paul returned to work, Jason and I returned to school. Jason was struggling and dabbling with marijuana in order to cope, but I was in denial. I do remember he had a photography elective that semester, and he told me his teacher called him up after class one day to tell him that he had also taught Eric, and that Jason had selected the exact same spot in class where Eric always sat. Those little things were big to us. Every reminder of what we once had with Eric felt meaningful and we tucked it all away in our hearts. We were each compartmentalizing our lives in order to function, some of it in healthy ways and some, not so much. My designated escape was school.

I lost myself in fourth semester of nursing school. There was something that rose up in me that said, "Everything has been taken from me, but not this. He cannot have my career too." I still had two finals to finish up from third semester, so I returned early to pass those in order to continue on. I had two classroom days and two clinical days a week at Valley Lutheran Hospital. I was given grace in other areas of my life but not with school, and I didn't expect it or want it. It was an extra weight to carry at the time, all the studying, and what I was subconsciously doing was pushing off the inevitable grief I would need to confront one day. Grief cannot be side-stepped indefinitely, but I was certainly going to try!

A couple of stories come to mind and they happened when I was a student nurse at the hospital. Once, a patient coded in the hallway. I realized he was dying and my reaction was pretty visceral. My instructor glanced over and saw my struggle and had another student whisk me off the floor. I had so much raw attachment to the weight of life and death during those early years, and there were times that being a nurse, even though I loved it, was tough. There was another day that the students were picking our patients from a roster and I noticed a patient named "Eric Edwards". One of my fellow students noticed me noticing and leaned over to say, "It's not him, Debbi, don't go look." I had to go look. The mind does funny things when it's searching for closure. As I was walking back from the room, my friend said, "You went and looked, didn't you?" I shook my head yes and the tears started flowing. The dam would break whenever it wanted, I didn't get to decide when my emotions were allowed to overcome me.

There were some positive things happening along with my focus on school. In March we terminated the lease on our apartment. The management was understanding of our unusual circumstances and we weren't penalized. For the first time in our lives, we were eager to get out of Mesa, the city we had known and loved since we were kids. We signed papers on a new construction home in Gilbert and it was completed in June. Jason would begin his sophomore year at Gilbert High School. This felt like a bit of a fresh start.

In May, I graduated with my RN. Everyone in the family attended the ceremony, and we went out for a nice dinner afterward. Perhaps they were surprised that I finished, considering the turn our life had taken. It would have been easier to step away or take a break and no one would have blamed me even one little bit, but I knew if I didn't return to school immediately, I never would. My mom and Paul "pinned me" and I was almost official. Valley Lutheran hired me even before graduation and I would be a "Nurse Intern" until I took my state boards in July. The state boards are intense for anyone, and for me they represented another big life change in a very short period of time. Bury a child, build a house, graduate from college, start a career. These are monumental life changes and here I was piling them on. I cried for two days. The whole process with the boards was so formal and intimidating and exhausting. And it was so quiet in there. I hated quiet more than anything because then the thinking took over. I thought about how I was ticking off my personal goals, but only one of my kids was there to see it. I was thinking about how Eric was supposed to watch me finish this and how he would have been proud of me. It was all so bittersweet. Several weeks later when I received that thin envelope in the mail, I knew I had passed the boards on my first try and that was satisfying.

I stayed at Valley Lutheran for only a few months. I was on the Renal Oncology floor and the constant loss of patients had me looking for a new opportunity. Within a few months, I ended up at Desert Samaritan in Labor and Delivery. Nurses see a lot and OB nurses see even more. The joy and elation when a happy, healthy family brings a happy, healthy baby into the world is magical. Ten little fingers and ten little toes and a blank slate that is all dreams and potential wrapped up in a tiny striped blanket? It's pure bliss. And most of them go just like that. Most times there aren't impossible problems. No one ever thinks, "This baby will leave this earth before me," but that happens too and it's called fetal demise. There is no easy way to tell a woman that her baby didn't make it. But, lo and behold, within about six months at Desert Samaritan, I was trained in the "Resolve Through Sharing" protocol that would allow me to follow these families for one year after their loss.

Friends, if you are ever in the Labor and Delivery unit of a hospital and you see a white rose on one of the doors just know that family is having a sad day. After the delivery, we would keep the baby in a warmer and then wrap them in warm blankets before placing them in mom's arms. The parents could hold the baby for as long as they wanted to, and when they were ready, we would wheel the whole warmer into the picture room. We had props that we would use like dad's wedding ring, a tape measure, tiny little knitted booties and hats. I was one-on-one with these families, and the goal was to help bring closure, or at least begin the process of healing by acknowledging these innocent souls who were too perfect for this world.

As you can imagine, sometimes people would ask what led

me to this exact role. They were curious about how someone ends up with such a gut-wrenching job and how I could possibly empathize with their loss. If they asked, I would tell them. I always matched their level of curiosity when it came to my story, and I only offered details if prompted. Because I would spend the next year in contact and we would begin to form a relationship, I was often asked, "Debbi, how many kids do you have?" I had two. Past tense. Some of them picked up on the context and some were too lost in their own emotions to notice. It was different because they were grieving potential and I was grieving reality, a half-finished life, but God gives us each grace to walk our own story and I had no desire to figure out whose heart was more broken. Empathy came easily for these families, and although it was a hard calling, I knew this was the right position for me.

That season of life was defined by my ability to compartmentalize. I could lead families through unspeakable pain, but after work, I would wander the grocery store for two hours and end up with an empty cart. In order to fall asleep, the TV needed to be on, and preferably set to a movie I had memorized. I didn't want to process anything new, I just needed to be lulled to sleep by familiarity and knowing "what would happen next" which is something movies can, but real life cannot deliver. In the mornings, I would finish my overnight shift and go to hearings at the courthouse in Mesa. So many hearings. Trust me when I share that real life is not like a true crime show you can watch on A&E. Those programs show the crime, an investigation, and then quickly cut to the trial and judgment. The reality is much more tedious and time consuming. It would take two years of pre-trial hearings to get us to trial.

I was a fish out of water when it came to the legal system and it was the State of Arizona who brought the case against Pete. I was just along for the ride. I had spent the past few years learning medical terminology, and that was finally familiar, but

I needed to buy books on the legal system to keep up. Hearings are what happen when a trial is pending. Every time there was new "discovery" in the case or the police got a warrant to seize something, there would be a new investigation focused specifically on that article. Normally the prosecution (our side) would submit new evidence, and the defense would call a hearing to try and disprove whatever was found. For example, there was an entire hearing about the seat cover from Eric's car. Eric's blood was on it, but the defense would still try to create doubt and confusion by questioning which seat it was on and whether it even existed. These hearings can be a little "crazy making" honestly, and they went on every couple of weeks for two full years. Hearings are in the morning before lunch and trials start after the break. The State of Arizona would mail us about a week in advance of each hearing, so we received a steady stream of mail from Victims Services for a couple of years.

Here's a funny story; the first time I went to a hearing, I had no idea what to expect. It didn't occur to me I would be going through security so my pockets were full of syringes and a pair of gauze scissors from work. I quickly learned the process; no needles and no scissors when going through security! If I remember right, you then look for your judge on a list so you know which courtroom to enter. I was a nervous wreck entering that courtroom the first few times. The room is full, lots of activity, attorneys roaming around consulting with their clients. The types of cases are mixed, in other words there may be people coming in off the street with minor crimes as well as prisoners coming in from the jail, all within that morning window. I didn't even sit down the first time I went. I didn't know where to sit and, I was taking it all in and observing the chaos that would eventually feel familiar.

After a few hearings, Pete realized who I was. I was the petite, middle aged nurse in scrubs who showed up for every hearing and was often speaking with the prosecutor. It wasn't too hard to figure out I suppose. From that day forward, Pete would spend the hearing making lewd gestures and mouthing profanities at me. He was trying to intimidate me and make me uncomfortable. It worked. When that started, our Marriage Accountability Group through church decided that someone would always attend court with me, for moral support. Once again, our tribe was coming through for us and we were so grateful.

Attorneys are a rare breed. The defense attorney assigned to Pete was fairly young, maybe in his late 30's. He was also a loud, cocky, narcissistic know-it-all who couldn't imagine losing a case. I don't know what kind of person you need to be to perform the duties of a public defender with so much passion when your client is clearly guilty. One day in court was particularly difficult. I believe this was during the trial, when a bullet-by-bullet timeline was constructed. When the court dismissed, I lost it and sobbing cries that only a mother would understand took over. My friend Lynn grabbed me, pulled me tight to her chest and let me unleash. The defense walked over to the prosecutor and said, "If she is still crying like this when the jury returns she will be out of here." I looked him right in the face with my bleary eyes and in my most defiant tone said, "I have 15 minutes and I will be fine." Maybe in his everyday life he was a decent guy, but in the courtroom that man was unbearable.

"Our" attorney (the state of Arizona) changed a couple of times. About a year into the hearings, we got a less experienced female attorney and I could see she was super nervous but I was impressed by her. I can't say for sure but I'm guessing this was her first capital murder case. She was a tough cookie, but she was kind to us. She even invited me to visit the DNA lab with her, which was very interesting. It seemed her confidence was building as the hearings continued to go in her favor and she ended up doing a fantastic job overall.

Over the two years of hearings, Jason's drug use was escalating.

I was the Queen of Denial and Fear at that point because the thought of one incident taking both of my children from me was too much to bear. Jason would eventually go into treatment, but that would not be until after the trial took place.

Finally, after all the stalling by the defense, they ran out of tactics and excuses for hearings and the trial was set to begin on October 28th, 1993. We were nervous but ready for some real progression in the case. We were ready to learn the fate of our son's killer.

6

The Trial

I WAS USED TO spending time in a courtroom and was no longer intimidated by the legal terminology or the hustle and bustle of that environment. But, as always, there were some things I was unprepared for because a trial is much different than a hearing.

Hearings move fast and their purpose is to determine what can or cannot be mentioned at trial. The defense will grasp at straws and search for evidence they want thrown out, never presented to a jury. For example, Pete's attorney was trying to eliminate his shoes and the footprint evidence at the scene from being used, because the shoes were taken "illegally". Never mind Eric's blood was all over those shoes. The final straw will be when the defense presents the offer to avoid trial altogether by their client pleading guilty to a lesser charge. This option may be presented as a way to "spare the family" the heartache of trial or to save the state resources or just to see if the family is content with the perpetrator simply behind bars. Pete could have pled guilty to second degree aggravated murder. In some cases this would make sense. But not in ours. We would be sticking with the first degree premeditated murder charge because we were confident we would "win" – which is a strange way to describe a process where there is nothing but loss.

Jury selection is an interesting process and one I had never taken part in before (and likely never will considering our life story). I had my sweet friend Lynn with me and she took copious and organized notes throughout what became a long day of interviews. My impression of the process goes something like this…

There is a huge pool of potential jurors, maybe up to 100 people to begin with. They have filled out questionnaires, which are used to reduce the pool down to a manageable number of candidates. Many people will be released based on their questionnaire answers and their civic duty is done for the time being. The second phase of jury selection will be extensive questioning of the candidates who remain, some examples include:

Do you have trouble seeing, hearing, or ambulating?

What is your occupation, specifically?

What are your religious beliefs?

Do you understand the possibilities of the sentencing in this case?

How do you feel about the death penalty? Because that is a possible outcome of this case.

Can you withstand the emotional rigors of what is ahead of you?

Do you understand this will be a six week trial?

Can you be objective?

The third phase of selection involves each attorney receiving a series of "strikes", where they can eliminate jurors for any reason or no reason at all. The defense would strike deep methodical thinkers like engineers and scientists, while the prosecution would strike compassionate people like nurses and teachers. Of course this is a huge over-generalization, and there is more method to that madness, but at the end of it all, the last phase of jury selection is when both parties somewhat agree upon 12 jurors and two alternates who "represent a cross-section of society". They will appoint a "leader" to speak on behalf of the group, and in our case, the representative was a younger gentleman who drove a Pepsi truck and made it obvious he absolutely did not want to be there! I should mention that this jury was not sequestered (meaning they went home to their families every evening and did not stay in a hotel). Mesa is a huge city and this was not considered a high profile case, so that precaution was not taken. They were however ordered to not discuss the case with anyone, and because one of them did, an alternate juror took their spot.

There is one interesting thing about the timing of our case. Bear with me as I explain, because it's both relevant and technical. Our crime was committed in December of 1991, just before victim's rights were overhauled in Arizona. At this time, a capital murder conviction would result in a 25-to-life sentence (with parole being an option of course) or the death penalty. Pete was grandfathered into this protocol even though our trial started much later. Another unique restriction under this "old" system, was that witnesses (even family) would not be able to sit and watch the trial before being called to testify.

Fast forward to January of 1992. Yes, just one month later. Victim's rights were implemented through a system called Truth in Sentencing and the new standard for a first degree premeditated murder was life in prison, no possibility of parole, and the possibility of the death penalty remained. Truth in Sentencing allows victim's families to breathe a little easier and not spend the rest of THEIR lives following the case because the sentence would be exactly as stated in court. Life meant life. There were two benefits to us under this new system. First, we were assigned a "Victim Advocate" and her name was Esther. Her title explained her role towards us; she would explain the process, giving us relevant information as things progressed. In addition, victims and family could now stay in the court room for the entire trial, regardless of when they testified.

Here was the daily routine: Paul would go to work in the mornings. My employer was kind enough to give me weekend shifts during the trial so I could attend daily. My friend would pick me up, both of us dressed semi-formally, and she would drive us to the courthouse at 1:00. We would clear security, double check the courtroom we were assigned to, and enter the fray. We would do this every weekday for six weeks. Wash. Rinse. Repeat.

Opening statements on the first day were quite theatrical. Almost (but not maybe as dramatic) as a crime television show. Both sides know this is their first opportunity to captivate the jury before they begin formulating opinions, and it's quite the show. There would be a monologue about both Pete and Eric, each of their attorneys trying to tug at the heart strings of the jury. The commonalities between the two boys were striking. Pete and Eric were both just beginning their lives, with so much promise ahead. They both had beautiful girlfriends and dreams for their futures. They both were imperfect but were figuring things out through trial and error as most young men do. The difference of course was that one of them, my child, was no longer with us. As the case was outlined from each side, the jury was listening intently, and I was trying to, but the whole thing was so surreal it was hard to believe my life had come to this.

At a hearing, the prisoners are obvious because they are chained and wearing their prison uniforms. At the trial, the prisoner will be dressed nicely as they are trying to make an impression on the jury. Pete's attorney would enter every day with a cart full of bank boxes that contained (their) evidence and case notes. The boxes were piled high, and Pete's trial clothes were always neatly folded on top. After the opening statements, the whole trial goes like this; prosecution, defense, prosecution, and then the judge has the last word. Because of this, some people may be asked to testify twice (I can't remember perfectly now, but I think Josh was asked to testify twice during the trial).

Here was a surprise. I was called as the prosecution's first witness. I was not expecting that and the victim's advocate program was so new that neither our attorney nor Esther had prepared me, but a warning would have been nice. A few things that were presented for me to validate as Eric's property were the rent check that was still in his pocket, as well as a ring that Shannon had given him. It was really hard to see a physical representation of things that were on my son's person during the last moments he was alive. I'm guessing those items went straight to an evidence locker and have long since been discarded, but even now I wish I had asked for that ring because I wanted it so badly.

Josh was also called early in the process. He was transported in his prison jumpsuit and still wearing it on the stand. By this time he was 19 or 20 and every bit the smart aleck kid he had presented before. No compassion. Unaffected. Seemingly no regrets. He was asked to clarify the timeline of events all over again, and his job as the prosecution's witness was to confirm Pete as the shooter (remember he had taken a plea deal to give Pete up).

Josh's mother was also called and I had such a heart for her. She had done the right thing over and over again (would I have been strong enough to do the same if the tables were turned?) and I knew she was broken over her son's choices. When Doris was being led out of the courtroom by Esther, we were just two moms each dealing with our own heartache and I smiled at her. It was genuine. Esther told me that Doris expressed her surprise by that, and I hope she knew that my hatred was never directed toward her.

Some of Eric's friends testified, some of Pete's friends did too…I won't remember them all. There were technical components to the trial in addition to more personal testimony. The day the bullet-by-bullet breakdown was covered was awful for me.

Josh was answering questions like, "Were his eyes open or closed in that moment?" and, "Was Eric speaking or was he silent at this point?" Ugh. Really tough.

The forensic doctor who did the autopsy had a drawing of Eric's body and he was demonstrating the trajectory of the bullets with props and a thorough explanation proving that the bullets absolutely came from the back seat. At one point, with gloves on, he was pulling Eric's clothing from a bag and he said, "You know this was infested with maggots, right?" And the nonchalant response was, "It's all been in the freezer so that's fine." He's thinking about the shirt in his hands. I'm thinking about my son, the priceless human being who wore that shirt. I understood why these things needed to be presented in such a matter-of-fact way, but knowing that didn't make it any easier to sit through.

There were also blood stain pattern analysts employed by each side and here is my perspective on that. Science is factual but the way its interpreted is subjective. Evidence can be manipulated and it often is. In a courtroom, the best show wins. This was hard for me, the back and forth with the scientific evidence. I realize that humans can have different thoughts, opinions and impressions of the same scenario but it seems like science should be a little less subjective. I tend to be more of a black and white person…there's not a lot of grey in my world. Grey is what I try to cover with love and grace. But the truth is the truth.

The prosecution rested after the final witness and it was time to move on to the defense.

The defense had its own roster of witnesses. Some were present, and some mailed letters to be shared. Friends, Pete's girlfriend, and his mother (who made a lot of excuses for him) were some of the witnesses. There were many times that Pete's girlfriend was the only person on his side of the courtroom. He had been locked up for two years already, and I wouldn't have expected much different. People move on, especially young people. The defense had its own forensic and blood spatter experts trying to disprove what ours had so obviously proven.

Then, Pete was up. I still hated him so much at that point that it was hard to see anything positive. Here was this huge man, tall, broad-shouldered and physically intimidating. But when he spoke, I had to admit that he was very intelligent, well-spoken and composed. His demeanor and his ability to communicate were totally misaligned with the stereotype of someone on trial for capital murder. There was one tiny shred of me that felt sad for him, someone so obviously intelligent had ruined his whole life. I couldn't look at him and not see my loss so I didn't really watch him, I stayed trained on the jury. It was me watching the jury watching the defendant and that's how it had to be.

The prosecution had gone much longer than the defense, but after the defense rested, the prosecution had one more shot at refuting some of their arguments, circling back to get clarification or disprove something that was said. Then, the prosecution rested for the last time.

The final step of the trial before the jury deliberates is when each attorney gives closing arguments. It's a lot like the first day's opening statements, those are the book-ends to the trial. They recap the case hoping to influence the jury one final time. And the format, once again, is prosecution, defense, and then prosecution with the last word.

It had been six long, grueling weeks and now our son's murderer was at the mercy of 12 strangers. This would be a first-degree-premeditated murder conviction or nothing at all. The judge would excuse the jurors to a room with very specific instructions, and we were sent to a family waiting room while they deliberated. After three or four hours, the jury came back with a unanimous guilty vote. I'm not sure who read the verdict. I was listening to the reader, but my eyes were glued on Pete. I was terrified that I would miss the word "not" and only hear the word guilty, just one of the tricks my mind was pulling on me. Pete stayed stoic throughout. I figured if he was "not guilty" he would have had some reaction so I was confident I heard correctly.

We all shuffled out of the courtroom, and Larry had us all circle up in the parking lot. A giant group of our supporters, family and friends who had seen us through two years of insanity were all present. He told us to hold hands and he would count to three. At the count of three, everyone was to scream at the top of their lungs for as long and as loud as they wanted to. It sounded silly but it was a fantastic release. We had been stuffing our emotions, waiting, being "courtroom quiet" and anticipating this day for so long, we needed to let it all out.

But, this was still not the end of the road. A separate court date was set for sentencing, and we would be waiting another three months to find out Pete's fate.

Finally, we re-convened for the sentencing. Prior to the judge announcing that Pete would be doing "25-to-life with the possibility of parole" we were able to read and share the family's impact statements. I put so much time and heart into constructing my impact statement but I realize no matter how passionate the statement, judges (unless they have been through this personally) can't understand how the murder of your child changes you. You only know if you know - and this is a small club that no one asks to join. I didn't have particular thoughts about Pete not receiving the death penalty, I didn't much expect that, but I did know two things; I wanted him locked up and the key thrown away, and I would fight against his parole if ever given the opportunity.

Without the trial looming over us, it would be time to give in to grieving. Of course, the process had already begun, but it is messy and there's no formula and the trial had been a distraction. Our little family would all handle the next many years and the grief process very differently. I'm so thankful for our faith, for without that, I don't know how a family goes through a loss like this. We were grateful that justice had been served, and that process was complete. At this point, none of us could have fathomed that the one thing that would become most important in our story was not justice, but mercy.

Discussion Questions
Part 2

1. Have you ever been to a funeral service for a child? How are the thoughts and emotions different from thoughts and emotions at services when the deceased enjoyed a full life?

2. What did you think about Debbi's "little miracles"? Have you ever received confirmation from the Lord, right when you needed it most?

3. Debbi's nursing career quickly involved working with families who lost their newborn babies. Why do you think she was drawn to this work, when she was still grieving her own loss?

4. How did you feel when Debbi described her initial softening toward Pete in the courtroom? She acknowledged that "his demeanor and ability to communicate were totally misaligned with the stereotype of a killer", and "she was sad that someone so obviously intelligent had ruined his whole life."

5. What do you think would have been a fair sentence for Pete? How do you feel about the death penalty in general? How about in this case?

PART THREE:

Healing

You are given the "magic eyes" to see the person who hurt you in a new light. Your memory is healed, you turn back the flow of pain and you are free again.

Adapted from: <u>Forgive and Forget</u> by Lewis B. Smedes

7

Confronting Grief

ENIAL. ANGER. BARGAINING. Depression. Acceptance. These are the stages of grief according to expert Elisabeth Kubler-Ross. These emotions are not linear or organized as we come to terms with our loss. We fade in and out of them without any real control over where our next stop will be or how long we will linger. Grief is a rollercoaster car that is often off its track or stuck at the top, just waiting for the drop that turns your world upside down all over again. Grief, as it turns out, is perpetual survival mode.

What happens when the death of your loved one is unexpected? Shock. It precedes denial. It's a prolonged, low-grade panic attack that causes you to lose track of time, fabricate story lines (turns out Eric was not in witness protection, nor was he a prodigal son who would come home soon for his celebration feast as if we never missed a beat). It had me disassociated from reality, responding inappropriately to appropriate situations, and feeling like I was floating untethered in a world that required my presence. Shock thoughts were like a monkey on my back, and I had to shake them off before I could even begin officially grieving.

I should reiterate that immediately after Eric's death and

through his funeral, I was in a protective bubble, surrounded by family and friends who handled nearly everything on our behalf. That was God's protection and provision. I don't know if I could have made the few decisions I was required to make, or have held myself together for the services if I weren't in that bubble of protection. The collision of thoughts when the human body is in shock is staggering, and it's difficult to explain, but it greatly impairs your decision making abilities. I would say it was about the time that I graduated school, that I also graduated "shock" and would then move on to denial.

In nursing school, toward the very end (after Eric was gone), it was time for my psychology class. It was a six week class that quickly included the stages of grief and the process of grieving. The "grief graphic" I'd printed out looked like a tidy little upside down bell curve. I really tried to approach this process in a scholarly way. I even posted the graphic on my refrigerator so I would be reminded, "This is what you are doing now, Debbi. You are grieving. If you study this model enough, you will get it right." I always got A's in everything that mattered. Best laid plans.

There were a few things I understood as I attempted to become a "student of grief:" I knew we would need support from other people who had experienced the murder of a child, I knew I would need to forgive Pete in order to fully accept this new life without Eric, and I knew that we had to (on a practical level) move along. We needed to work and raise Jason and try to experience our own lives; it would not honor Eric to dwell.

But I dwelled. The pain was constant. My identity was "the mom of the murdered child," and I spoke about it way more than I should. Maybe my words would help people understand my pain and how much my life had changed. Maybe I just needed to continue processing it externally to wrap my own mind around it. I went to the grave four or five times a week for the first year or two. I would take a tiny little broom with me and whisk the grave off and check to make sure the flowers looked nice. I never stayed very long, but I think this process helped negate my denial. This is real. This is your son's grave site. His name is on the marker. He is in the ground. I needed that visceral connection of physically being there where I was not distracted and could not pretend that this was all a nightmare. Even though this loss was running my life, I still needed convincing that it was true.

Esther (our advocate in the trial) suggested we attend a Parents of Murdered Children group. The format is much like any support group where everyone tells their story, guest speakers are invited, and people share updates and breakthroughs they have had. The difference with this group is that the anger in the room is palpable and maybe even celebrated. Because it is absolutely justified. Each of these families had a child taken from them in the coldest way possible. I realized fairly quickly that anger is not where I land, it's not my "besetting sin" and although I had no judgment for those parents, I couldn't bear the intensity of those meetings. We only returned a few times over the years, mostly down the road when we were asked to share our story. During the earliest part of our journey, we felt more comfortable processing our questions and expressing our grief with friends and confidants at church. When given the opportunity to come and share, we would point the parents in the meetings to Jesus. I'm certain that sounded over-simplified at times, but He was all we had and He was all we needed. I hope at least some of the parents we met through the years turned to Him in their time of greatest need.

Here is a funny story about anger, from someone who suppressed the expression of it for so long: One day I was vacuuming the house and this demure, level-headed, "sweet Christian mom" began cussing up a storm. The vacuum was roaring and under the cover of the commotion I was really giving Pete a piece of my mind. A few hours later as I reflected on that out-of-body-like experience, I thought, "Wow! Debbi! You did it! You did anger! You checked the anger box!" I really believed I would never do anger again. Until the next time, of course.

When I did circle back to anger, it usually looked more like indignation and sometimes it came out at the wrong time and place. I was upset at "systems." I was upset when someone receiving medical care didn't get (in my opinion) enough advocacy. I was upset at the Mesa Police Department. I was really upset when they compared my Eric to boys like Pete and Josh, or when they referred to teenagers as a "pack of dogs." That felt especially offensive. The police didn't care that Eric had been raised in the church. They didn't acknowledge that his mom and dad were married and stable and happy. They didn't even ask if he was allowed to run the streets – he wasn't – they just assumed it. Those things frustrated me. I suppose it was easier to "get mad" at things that were less consequential than it was to confront all the emotions I was avoiding.

Anger turned inward leads to depression, and there are a lot of things I could share about depression. In fact, it wasn't new to me at all. Throughout my life, depression came in waves. The bouts after Eric's death were tidal waves. I had previously been on a medicine called Elavil for depression. The 10 mg. dose I was given was tiny, but it still knocked me on my butt. After Eric's death, my doctor increased it to 150 mg. overnight and I was handling it well. As expected my nervous system was nearly inconsolable. One day I was driving down Main Street, headed toward the cemetery. I would often cry and drive, and this particular day, I was sobbing. Breathless, I was crying out to the Lord, "I can't do this. I can't live like this. God, help me." It was like the Lord himself spoke a pep talk to my soul, and I was back on track for a bit. The roller coaster would re-visit depression often over the years, and I would use a combination of medication and therapy to try and manage it, with varying degrees of success. One thing was certain, regardless of anything else I tried, I always landed in the arms of Jesus.

The only stop my roller coaster didn't make was "bargaining". There was nothing to bargain. Bargaining is certainly its own version of hell that people resort to when their loved one is terminal and their suffering is prolonged. I don't know if one is better or worse, but in my experience, shock and bargaining don't exactly co-exist. You either don't know you will soon lose someone you love, and your life is changed in an instant, or you know it all too well, and you are bargaining with them or bargaining with God for them to stay a little longer. Each are horrible in their own ways.

Acceptance is not the same as forgiveness, and I like to acknowledge both. Acceptance will come later in my story. Forgiveness will come first on a cerebral level, and eventually it would take over my whole heart. As a Christian, I know forgiveness. My life is built on "being forgiven," and I know the importance of modeling Jesus by forgiving others. I knew immediately after Eric died that I would need to forgive Pete, eventually. Did I care? Not yet. I kept it in the recesses of my mind. Somewhere during this time, my friend Wendy said to me, "Debbi, if you ever want to go see Pete in prison, I'll go with you." What a strange thing to say. The only reason to go see Pete would be if I had forgiven him, which I knew would come one day, but I had no desire to tell him in person and open the door to reconciliation, which in my mind was the restoration of a lost relationship. We never had a relationship to begin with, and I had no plans to start one now. Absolutely not. Some things are impossible.

So, those are the stages of grief, and experiencing each of them deeply as I went through them repetitiously is imperative and painful beyond words. A couple of my favorite phrases are "feelings buried alive never die" and "the body keeps score." Both are true. I would eventually battle weight gain, autoimmune issues and debilitating migraines as I continued revisiting denial, anger and depression over the years.

As I mentioned before, we were each going through this process individually. Grief just takes over and you're on the ride. But you are not on the same ride as your family. Sometimes you are not even at the same park. Jason was so young and impressionable and fragile when Eric's life was taken. A kid his age has no coping skills - that muscle builds over time - and this about took him out. Jason's drug use escalated from marijuana into methamphetamines. There were rehab stints and times he was missing (can you even imagine my heart?) and me finding him practically unconscious and emergency doctor visits. It was just a horrible season. This was his way of coping. I knew why and I knew it all too well. I also knew that "tough love" may be the answer, but I couldn't do it.

If I wasn't missing Eric, I was hating Pete. If I wasn't missing Eric or hating Pete, I was worrying about Jason. My thoughts were completely consumed by three young men, all for different reasons. Paul probably could have done "tough love," and Jason likely would have been better for it, honestly. I enabled some weird behaviors during this season because I was terrified of losing my only living son. No one could reason with me that Jason would be alright, because trauma ruled this area of my life. In my mind I had already lost one child, and there was no guarantee I could keep the other one. Bad things happen, we were proof, and I was desperate and terrified, thinking always of death and loss.

Jason's addiction would span a big piece of our lives, and it was so difficult, but before I move on I want to share that after rehab with Salvation Army, Jason's life was back on course. I cannot say enough good things about that program, and I am eternally grateful to them. Jason is the most loving, kind, caring son I could ask for. He never intended to hurt me or anyone else when he began coping with Eric's death by escaping through drugs. The fallout of a tragedy like ours can be messy and destructive, but with God's help and the love of a family, we do recover!

The year was now approaching 2004. Approximately 10 years had passed since the trial ended. We had moved through a lot of pain with a lot of help and we still had a long way to go, but something was beginning to shift in my heart. Our church life was such an incredible blessing and support. We had friends at our workplaces, but church was where we were truly understood. Our friend Larry had a lot of wisdom, and some things he shared with us resonated deeply. Looking back, there were a couple of conversations that were transformative for me:

One day we were talking about Eric's return to church shortly before his death, even commenting on his desire to bring others. I was slightly offended when Larry said, "Oh. That's called 'Dying Grace' and there was a book written about it." He then went on to explain that while I was simply happy Eric was changing his ways, it was deeper than that. The Lord was preparing Eric to meet Him. I didn't much like that explanation, it rubbed me the wrong way at the time. But since then, I have seen it happen over and over with others, and I have come to accept it – God wants His people with Him and He will move on our hearts when our time on this earth is drawing near.

The Lord is not slow in keeping His promise, as some understand slowness. Instead He is patient with you, not wanting anyone to perish, but everyone to come to repentance. 2 Peter 3:9 NIV

Another Larry-ism was, "There is an end to grief, but you will never be the same. You get to choose to be bitter or be better." I began to consider the challenge of getting better, and I knew that forgiveness was my path forward, but I was in no hurry.

8

Spiritual Shifts

ONE YEAR BLURRED into the next. 24 hours never passed that I didn't think about Eric, but the thoughts of him were consuming less of my life, and my soul no longer felt crushed. I thought my heart was healed, but maybe it was just scabbed over. The adage "time heals all wounds" was not exactly accurate, but it is true that details get foggy as time marches on. You can't keep your pain and anguish at a 100/10 all the time… it will exhaust you and everyone around you. So, we were normal people leading normal lives, except for our "watershed moment" that would mark us for the rest of time.

In 2004, we felt called to relocate again, this time to the Queen Creek area. At the time it was an up and coming community where our church had received land to eventually build a "daughter church." In the meantime, every week, we would set up a portable fellowship in the elementary school across the street. If you have ever been part of a plant like this, bless you! It is not easy and it's not for the weary. But we were younger then and excited to see God working in this new area. Paul was on the board, and had lots of contact with the pastor. When the pastor shared that he would be building a house in the area, we decided to offer ours up so they could move sooner. So, we shared our home with a family of five, including small children, for many months! Our pastor's wife was a trained counselor and would often talk to me or give me literature about "forgiveness." I would say at this point I had achieved forgiveness on a cerebral level and when I read those handouts, they would mostly confirm all the progress I had made and occasionally challenge me a bit. Maybe she saw something in me that I didn't recognize at the time because I thought I was doing great. Little did I know there would be much more forgiving to come, but that would be years in the making.

Paul was working as an estimator for State Farm in Tempe. He opted for a 10-7 schedule to avoid the heavy commuter traffic. Paul hates traffic! If you know anything about metro Phoenix, you know that Queen Creek is at least 45 minutes from Tempe. We both spent a lot of time in the car because of our jobs (I have to admit I did not despise it as much…it was my time for worship music and reflection).

I was working as an OB Peds RN Case Manager for Banner Health Plans. That is quite a title, and what it indicated was that all those years delivering babies had begun to wear me out and I applied for a change. This was the perfect job for me in what I refer to as "the Golden Age of managed care," when there were people like me between the doctors and insurance providers, advocating for the patient. I managed high risk OB patients, 60-100 at a time. I contacted them after each appointment and made sure they and their growing babies got the best care possible. One time, I was even able to relocate a family to Arizona in order to prevent a fetal crisis, and that patient sent me the sweetest "thank you" gift. It was rewarding work; I would stay in it for many years and eventually retire from this role.

Jason had gone to school to become an electrician. He was staying sober, which made us proud, and he did meet someone and marry in October of 2005. They bought a house and built a life apart from us, and our relationship was good. The marriage didn't make it, which was sad for everyone, but supporting our only living son through life's challenges has always been a priority. Jason and his wife did not have children, and my dream of becoming a grandmother slipped away.

Through the years, Victim's Services kept us informed of every event that pertained to our case. There were less all the time (Josh had been released; Pete had stopped getting "corrective actions" regularly) and it was a little quieter on that front. Our responsibility was to keep our address current with Victim's Services, and honestly I forgot to do this when we moved to Queen Creek. That could be construed as a win in some ways, meaning that so many positive life events were happening for us and around us that it slipped my mind. The other thing is that I had learned how to navigate the DOC system online so I could look things up any time I wanted to, and I did that on occasion. In any event, I forgot.

There were some really wonderful opportunities during those "empty nest" years. I was able to travel often with a good friend, while Paul honed his archery skills. He even went hunting in Africa (twice!) and has many trophies covering the walls of our living room that showcase his talent. We were serving in our church and had settled into this new community, most of whom had no idea who Eric was or what our family had been through. I had been challenged to pray for Pete and I committed to it. At first it was awkward and uncomfortable, but over time it got easier to pray for him. When I prayed for him, I envisioned him in prison. Always in prison.

Around 2008, I was again reflecting heavily on forgiveness. I had been asked to share at a women's event and give my testimony, which I was always glad to do, but I needed to revisit my thoughts in order to prepare the talk. I'm not proud of one statement I made, one that I now totally disagree with. "Everyone says you know you have forgiven if you can wish that person well - and I don't believe that is true." I said this unapologetically and from behind a pulpit and I wish I hadn't, but hindsight is 20/20. That's simply where I was at the time. Wishing him well felt like a betrayal to Eric, so I needed to reserve that one thing in Eric's honor. I did have other good insights to share and I hope the Lord filtered my message straight to each recipient's heart (I had come really far in my healing but it was clearly incomplete).

To be clear, we never thought Pete was outside of God's reach. Sometimes I would think about the prison ministries that may have reached Pete for Jesus, and I was good with the idea of spending eternity together. But I had no desire to wish him well or reconcile with him on this side of Heaven. We have known since we met Jesus that Heaven is full of sinners saved by grace and that humans were created for Heaven. I can honestly say that we didn't want an earthly reconciliation with Pete, but we did want the Lord to move in his life, absolutely no reservations about that.

Eventually, we felt like it was time to move along from the church we had helped plant. We searched for years, looking for a good fit (a friend of mine calls this "church dating" - looking for a place to settle in). Our faith was never shaken, our hope was always in Jesus, but we were a little displaced. On Sundays we would often check out different churches and then I would occasionally treat myself to an afternoon movie. Sometimes we would attend one fellowship for long stretches, up to a year at a time. But nothing felt like "home," and that was frustrating.

This season went on and on and I think it was 2017, when the Lord started moving on my heart again and this is also when I stumbled into what I call "the basement church". It was kind of a small, odd situation, but I was drawn there one Sunday and I brought a fresh notebook, turned to page 1. I sat down, unsure, questioning my choices, tired of church dating and longing for community once again. Before the service started, I felt like the Lord was speaking to me:

"I am not calling you here for what you think you can get."

That's it. That's all He said. I wrote it in my notebook. It's the only thing I wrote that day because the rest of the service we were watching some Californians perform - rapping and miming - all for Jesus of course. And the craziest thing about the "basement church" experience? I decided to go back. I figured I should go ahead and find out why He did call me there…and I knew this first visit with rappers and mimes probably wasn't it.

Around the same time, I was invited to a women's event at a friend's church. The guest speaker was a young lady who was confined to a wheelchair because of a medical mistake. While she was sharing, she was so upbeat and didn't seem a bit angry. I knew when I left the church that day that something had shifted within me on a spiritual level, and I knew that I was supposed to go visit Pete in prison. I didn't know what that would look like, but I called my friend Wendy (the one who said she would go with me if I ever decided to do this) to confirm that she was still willing. She reinforced that she was good to go, and she prayed for me. The Lord was layering up my circumstances as He tends to do. There are seasons of "dry and quiet" and there are seasons when it rains. This was becoming a season of rain.

As I mentioned before, I had not updated our address with Victim's Services so when Pete went up for his 25 year parole hearing (also in 2017), we did not know about it. Sometime later, I was poking around the internet and found the audio of that hearing. I listened to the entire thing online. Pete's parole was denied and I was relieved.

I did not know it yet, but radical changes were just around the corner for me. God was about to take me on the journey that would become my testimony. In His perfect timing, He would exchange beauty for ashes, triumph for tragedy, and gladness for mourning. Unimaginable freedom was the next stop on my roller coaster life, and finally "something good" would be the big, unbelievable focus of my heart.

> *"The Spirit of the Lord GOD is upon Me,*
> *Because the LORD has anointed Me*
> *To preach good tidings to the poor;*
> *He has sent Me to heal the brokenhearted,*
> *To proclaim liberty to the captives,*
> *And the opening of the prison to those who are bound;*
> *² To proclaim the acceptable year of the LORD,*
> *And the day of vengeance of our God;*
> *To comfort all who mourn,*
> *³ To console those who mourn in Zion,*
> *To give them beauty for ashes,*
> *The oil of joy for mourning,*
> *The garment of praise for the spirit of heaviness;*
> *That they may be called trees of righteousness,*
> *The planting of the LORD, that He may be glorified." Isaiah*
> *61:1-3 NIV*

9

Radical Forgiveness

I WAS STILL ATTENDING the "basement church" because the Lord told me I was there for a reason and I hadn't figured that reason out yet. All these years I had been trying to follow His lead. Listen to His voice. Go where He sent me. All these years I had seen Him in the messiness of my life, working, moving, and healing. And all these years I felt justified in my desire to forgive Pete, maybe even meet up with him in the safety of a prison, but never to reconcile. Ever.

Imagine my surprise when a sermon that I hated, I mean really hated, was one of the catalysts to my freedom. The pastor was speaking on "reconciliation" and it was awful. I was angry and crying and I felt so alone with that word that continued to plague me. After the service I confronted him and said, "Reconcile means to restore a previous relationship, yes?" His answer was odd. "You sure about that?" It all felt so personal and like I was being attacked, and I was fit to be tied. Why was the "R word" coming up again? Hadn't I done enough?

Life can change in an instant. Ours had. And mine would again.

Shortly after the "pastor made me mad," I was back for

another try. I still didn't know what my reason for being there was, but I am obedient to the Lord and He brought me back there once again. I was listening to a sermon with no relevance to this part of my life, and this will sound odd, but as the pastor was talking, I felt something lift off of me. It was as if a heavy blanket was peeled from the bottom of my toes to the top of my head. After the service was over, and I was making my way out to my car, something came over me. It overtook me. I was leveled emotionally and spiritually as I completely and totally forgave Pete in a moment. It wasn't optional and it wasn't logical, but it was a real and raw, undeniable reality that the last piece of unforgiveness I had harbored and withheld was now purged out of my entire being and replaced with pure love. I understood everything. I saw Pete as God saw me. The depths of my mercy and compassion for Pete were immeasurable as I acknowledged that his 20 year old brain wasn't developed when he made this choice that altered the course of so many lives. I blasted through thoughts of motive and consequences and justice and forgiveness and desperation and identity. Everything came together faster than I could actually process it. It was irrational and unhinged and unexpected and beautiful. It was just as messy as the rest of my life had been, but it was a gorgeous disaster that I could not contain.

I tried to steady myself as I let this wash over me. It was a tsunami of emotions unlike anything I had imagined possible. Even today, I struggle finding the right words to describe it! I sat in my car and experienced joy for the first time in my life. I didn't want to move. I didn't want to drive. I didn't want to risk losing it. I wanted to savor this feeling and never let it go. Now, here is the crazy part. This would last for the next several years. I felt light and free and all the anguish that had defined so much of my life was gone. Just…gone. I was truly soaring. I knew the forgiveness was authentic because I could finally and truly wish Pete well.

I got home and Jason and Paul were there. I sat down on the couch and casually announced, "I forgave Pete and I'm going to pursue meeting up with him." The guys were like, "Uh-huh, okay, that's great." But there was a fire inside of me that they weren't experiencing and although I am normally a mellow person, when I get determined there is no stopping me. Jason and Paul had forgiven Pete in their own ways long ago, and they were not going to be on this exact journey with me. And that was fine. I was prepared to do it alone, and so I dove right in, assuming and expecting we would be having our meeting in prison in no time at all.

The next day, Monday, I logged into the DOC system. It had been a while. I knew Pete had moved around several times, so I wanted to see which facility he was currently in (because I WAS going to see him soon). I had his DOC number memorized, and it was not pulling anything up when I typed it in. Perplexed, I decided to click the "inactive" button and there it was. The wind left my sails. The rug was pulled out from under me. I felt deflated. Pete had been discharged to house arrest on November 16th, 2017. How? The last I heard, his parole was denied. I still wanted to meet with him, but I had envisioned that meeting happening behind bars. How would this work now that he wasn't?

I found the muddled audio of the hearing and listened carefully. The conditions of his parole to house arrest were: no alcohol use, follow all mandatory DOC conditions and sanctions, random drug and alcohol testing, must not operate a motor vehicle, no contact with the victim's family, must pay restitution, obey all institutional rules, and transition to a halfway house (Old Pueblo in Tucson). There would be a $65 per month supervision fee and he would wear an ankle bracelet.

When asked, "Do I need to repeat these conditions to you again?"

He replied, "No sir I heard them clearly," and that got a little chuckle.

When wished "good luck" and notified this was the plan for the next six months, Pete replied, "Yes sir, thank you for the opportunity; I will not let you or anyone else down."

I was surprised and this felt surreal but I could not be deterred for long. I called Victim's Services and learned that my address in the system was old and that there was an attempt to notify me of the hearing that occurred but the mail was "returned to sender." So, I updated my contact info, got that squared away, and then boldly stated that I would need information to get in touch with Pete. "You see, I've got to meet with him! I've forgiven him and I'm supposed to tell him face to face! God took my hatred and my pain and he redeemed it! I see Pete as God sees me! Please help me!" Did I sound a little loony? Yes, indeed I did, but I didn't care. The young lady on the phone was very kind but her authority ended with giving me the phone number for his parole officer and the parole officer's boss. The parole officer's mailbox was always full. I never could get through. I finally called her boss. I told him who I was and what I was trying to do, to which he yelled, "WHY WOULD YOU WANT TO DO THAT? YOU CAN'T DO THAT! WE DON'T DO THAT!" He was so angry and I was so calm when I stated, "I will keep looking. Thank you."

God bless the internet. For all the messes it causes, social media has been a blessing in so many ways. The first thing I did was look for Pete on Facebook and Instagram. Bingo. There he was. His tag line was "Out From the Void and Better Than Ever," which confirmed I had the right guy. I discovered he was married and had a child and even a grandchild. I had so many questions. So I sent him a message, no biggie.

"My name is Debbi Edwards, do you know who I am?"

"Yes, I think so, how are you?"

"I would like to meet with you. Are you open to that?"

"Is this Debbie from high school?"

"My name is Debbi Edwards. Eric Edwards is my son."

ONE NANO SECOND PASSED BEFORE I WAS BLOCKED.

(Looking back I realize he was obeying the condition of his parole and he may have even thought I was trying to trap him or get him in trouble and that was probably terrifying for him...he did the right thing by blocking me.)

2018 and 2019 I was gathering info, researching things, reading online articles. I had run a parallel investigation to the cops when Eric was missing, and I could do it again. I knew from the hearing that Pete was living at "Old Pueblo" in Tucson, which is re-entry housing for the homeless, recently released prisoners, veterans, etc. I was pretty intense in my research, and it had begun to consume a lot of my time. Speaking of time, I thought I had all the time in the world to work my plan. Little did I know, life would change again with the Covid 19 pandemic that began in March of 2020.

2020 and its' aftermath...how does one describe something that not only changes your life, but the lives of everyone around you? Covid changed education, entertainment, healthcare, the church, family relationships, commerce, the prison system (many prisoners were released because the virus was so contagious and overcrowding was a danger). It changed the way we viewed our friends and neighbors. It changed politics and the economy. It was so divisive. We knew this was a strange time to be alive because the whole world was on "hold". The same office where I once did case management was now being used to assemble and distribute face masks through Banner Healthcare. Paul and I went to help with the efforts as well. I didn't have the thought to continue on my quest to connect with Pete because opportunities we once took for granted were now disregarded. I had been forming a plan for two years, and it just disappeared. I was still riding the wave of my forgiveness experience, and I still felt healthy, free and happy, but we were living in a world of "cant's" and "don't even try's." I hadn't given up on the idea that as long as it's possible to assure someone you have forgiven them, you should. But I shelved that dream for the moment.

Eventually, life got to a post-Covid "new normal" and we were notified of a hearing in March of 2024. Pete had requested "absolute discharge" which is basically an early termination from parole. His sentence would normally mean court involvement for a lifetime - after release he would forever be on parole – but it was within his rights to request absolute discharge, making him as free as you and me. And he took the chance.

This hearing was reminiscent, but not the same as, our previous court experiences. When we arrived we passed through security, and we signed in directly under Pete. He had arrived before us, and that was a weird moment to see his name there in writing, by his own hand, maybe only minutes before us. There was a panel of three judges and other court officials in the room. I had a Victim's Services advocate right next to me, and she was fantastic. The victims and perpetrator were kept completely apart and separated the entire time (we could watch as Pete and his witnesses spoke on a small closed circuit TV).

Pete would go first. The judges had many questions for him. They went around and around asking him "why" he did this to Eric, and he somberly said each time, "I had no reason to do this. It was senseless, it was immature, it was tragic, and I would take it back if I could." He came across as humble, gracious, educated (even a published author through a program at the University of Arizona). He never once tried to blame-shift or minimize the atrocity of his actions. He shared that it was about 10 years into his sentence that he took full responsibility for his past and his future and decided to change his ways. He became a model prisoner, pursued educational opportunities within, and refused to engage in the politics of prison life. He had glowing reviews from both a parole officer and one of the correctional officers who had worked with him in prison (she essentially said "the man you hear speaking right now is the same man I knew behind bars for many years; this is not an act"). He stated clearly that the State of Arizona had given him opportunities for which he was grateful, and that regardless of the outcome of this hearing, he would still pursue the honorable and productive path he was on. He spoke thoughtfully, considering and clarifying the questions he was asked before he answered them. He impressed me. Truly. He was essentially the system's "golden child" in that he embraced and pursued rehabilitation when most men in his situation would have stayed angry, hateful, and violent.

Although I didn't connect it at the time, I mentioned earlier that I felt my heart beginning to shift toward forgiveness around the 10-year-mark. I find it so befitting that it was also around that 10-year-mark that Pete's heart began shifting. Both of us would soon leave our old selves, our old patterns and habits behind and seek something better for our futures.

Paul would start when it was the victim's turn to share. He was angry! He didn't live in anger on a day-to-day basis, but he was (rightfully so) against Pete's absolute discharge and had a lot to say about that. He shared a picture of Eric, spoke of all the things and people who were impacted by this loss, and shared frustration that Pete was able to parade his achievements in front of everyone who would listen. Achievements that Eric never had the opportunity to experience. Children that Eric never got to have. Education he never got to pursue. And then there was Jason's addiction. He did share with the room that our marriage had survived "against all odds" and shared statistics that most couples that experience such a violent crime against their child will eventually divorce. He attributed our success to our faith, which is squarely where the credit should go. I was proud of Paul. He was speaking from his heart and saying how he felt, and he was well within his rights to do so.

On the other hand, I opened my time with, "We were told early on that we would never be on the same page at the same time, and no truer words were ever spoken." I expressed that I had forgiven Pete and that I didn't care if he was discharged or not. Truly. I repeated over and over that all I had wanted for the past six years was to talk to him. In person. And that every barrier placed in my way only made me more determined. I shared that on June 19th, 2018, I had written him a 12 page letter and mailed it to Victim's Services to forward to him. I enclosed the letter in a card that essentially said, "These are a lot of words. I know that. I poured out my heart. The bottom line is, I forgive you and I would like to meet with you so I can tell you that in person." Pete said later in this hearing that he never received that letter, and I still don't know what to think about that. He also said he had heard I wanted to meet with him, maybe from his parole officer? I told the judges that I had tried and tried to make a meeting happen for years, but that 2020 had derailed things. I even shared for some comic relief, "There were times I wondered how far I could push this and keep myself on the right side of the law. I thought about private investigators and showing up to parks in Tucson and all kinds of crazy things. Oh, the irony of wondering what defined 'stalking' when it comes to connecting with your son's killer. I literally felt like I had God's stamp of approval to pursue this and I still want it. Judges, I desperately want to meet with Pete in person."

Pete was given another opportunity to answer a few more questions. This time they were mostly about his work in construction, how often he thinks about his crime, how he functions in the community, and whether or not he has ongoing counseling. His answers to this set of questions were as eloquent and detailed as the first. He was grateful for his work, honest about his past, and encouraging others to pursue a straight and narrow path. He shared that he is married, and that he and his wife are committed to a healthy and supportive marriage, and a simple life.

The judges came back with their determination regarding total discharge. Ultimately, he was denied. He would stay on parole with minimal supervision, and he was advised to try again for total discharge in 2-3 years. He was doing all the right things; they just thought it was too soon. But another big decision was put on record that day, and the judge dictated the official verbiage lifting the victim contact," All conditions to remain the same with the exception:

"At the victim's request, the no contact condition is removed. Any contact with the victim (collectively Mrs. Edwards, Mr. Edwards or both) must be initiated by the victim and is in the victim's discretion. ADCRR is to look into the possibility of facilitating victim contact in a therapeutic setting."

It took six years, but finally my goal was a real possibility! After this, the judges asked to spend some time with me and Paul. They were interested in our story; however, there was a statement I overheard between the security guard and the Victim's Services lady. He said, "After Pete leaves, keep them here for a little bit. He's a big guy." So, they showed interested in my work (I had shared about using my experience of losing a child to comfort families who had lost their child). They showed interest in a book Paul brought in which our story was featured. They showed interest in my ability to forgive and move forward. We spoke for about an hour. During that hour, Pete was putting miles between us and almost all the way back to Tucson. He had slipped through my fingers, again.

Discussion Questions
Part 3

1. What do you think happens when we deny ourselves the grieving process? Is it possible to avoid grieving entirely? To what detriment, if any?

2. Have you ever heard the term "dying grace"? Have you seen it occur?

3. Debbi said she could see herself spending eternity with Pete, and hoped he had been reached through Prison Ministries. Did that surprise you? Why?

4. Have you ever stayed in a situation you didn't understand, until the reason was revealed? What if Debbi had left "the basement church" sooner? Do you believe God would have used another setting to orchestrate radical forgiveness within her?

5. The judges, parole officer, Paul, and even Pete had a hard time believing that Debbi should want to meet with Pete in person. What are your thoughts on her tenacity in pursuing a meeting?

PART FOUR:

Coming Together

You invite the person who hurt you back into your life; if he/she comes honestly, love can move both of you toward a new and healed relationship.

Adapted from: <u>Forgive and Forget</u> by Lewis B. Smedes

10

The Meeting

I LEFT THAT HEARING in March of 2024 with four business cards - two for Parole Officers, one for a Victim's Services Advocate, and one for the head of Victim's Services for the State of Arizona. Each of these people had direct access to Pete, and I truly thought setting up this long awaited meeting would be no big deal. I should clarify it was "long awaited" for me…six years I had been aching to see this happen, and thinking about it nearly constantly…but it was new information for (almost) everyone else. Most of them could not begin to conceive why this was so important to me or wrap their minds around something that I had been processing for years.

I called our advocate almost immediately to ask, "When and where?" I was so eager to get this meeting arranged and it felt like it was right in front of me. Imagine my dismay when the advocate said, "Both parties would normally go through a training prior to this. Also, it's never been done out of prison. The entire protocol we normally follow does not perfectly apply to you, but it seems some training would be beneficial." Evidently, everyone was skeptical about this meeting except for me. I politely declined training that would further delay the process, and we began working out the logistics of our meeting, which consumed much of April and May. I made it clear, "I will go anywhere at any time. I can go to Tucson. I'll stay in a hotel the night before and be available first thing in the morning. I'll make this convenient for Pete, and for everyone involved, I promise." All the signs were pointing to this shaping up for June, but no date had been set.

Then, again, my hopes were dashed. Pete's parole officer called me with the message, "Pete has backed out. He changed his mind." The first thing I said was, "Make sure he knows Paul isn't coming!" She assured me he knew that, but she promised to make it clear, just in case seeing Paul was the thing holding him back.

I was so mad. He didn't get to break this promise! It felt so unfair to wait six years for a meeting, only to have it within reach and then snatched away from me. I called the head of Victim's Services and expressed my frustration, but I had to acknowledge this is not something that can be forced. I knew the day I forgave him that I would meet him in person, but that did not seem to be the case any longer. I decided with or without a meeting, the forgiveness remained genuine, so I needed to put this down - for now. I had waited before and I could wait again.

By then, my sweet friend Wendy had passed. I really could have used her to help talk me through this. She was the one who had been by my side as I processed everything related to our case, forgiveness, and my desire to meet Pete. Wendy was gone, and I was left to my own ideas, some of which were admittedly desperate (calling Old Pueblo to try and enlist some help, figuring out where he lived in Tucson and "bumping into" each other, just generally bad ideas all around). I ruminated for about a week, talked myself out of all the dumb ideas I had, and decided to try something that made a lot more sense. Facebook.

When you aren't "friends" with someone on Facebook, you can still send them a "message request," so my next step was to try and make contact this way. The message I sent said something like:

I am so disappointed that you have changed your mind about meeting with me. This is the most important thing in the world for me, and I have been fighting for it for six years. I honestly think what I have to say would be beneficial for you as well, not just for me. This is very important. Will you please reconsider?

There were big things going on in our family that summer. My sister Vicki was dying from ALS. Our family made plans to get together with Vicki one last time and the date was set for a final farewell on Saturday, August 17th up in Northern Arizona. When I got notice that Pete had changed his mind and our meeting was back on the table for August 19th in Tucson (Southern Arizona), I didn't hesitate to confirm that this would be fine. I would criss-cross the entire state in the span of 48 hours for two of the most important days of my life. I said goodbye to Vicki, after I told her that Jesus and I loved her. I then picked up my sister Cathy, and we headed to Tucson. We would get a hotel on Sunday night the 18th and the next morning, I would finally say hello to Pete, and tell him the same - that Jesus and I loved him. Loving people and telling them about Jesus had always been the objective of my life and the most reassuring gifts I could offer anyone, under any circumstance. Why should these encounters be any different?

Cathy and I went to scope things out the night before the meeting. That has always been my style, to get familiar with the location of things and try to head off anything unknown. As I'm sure is clear by now, most often surprises in my life had not been so good. So, we found the complex where we would be meeting in the morning. It was surrounded by tall fences topped with barbed wire, and it had a large white rock with blue lettering outside of its gate, "Every Crime Has a Victim". Indeed.

When we arrived in the morning, Cathy and I were still sitting in the car when I quietly whispered, "Maybe we just drive home."

I didn't mean it, it was only a blip in time when I realized the moment I had built up to was upon me and I had no idea how this would actually go. Fantasies and reality can be so far apart. A couple of people from Phoenix had driven up to meet me, a parole officer and another person from DOC. They met us in the parking lot and ushered us through the gates that were now propped open. We stood inside the gate for a moment talking, and Cathy noticed before I did that Pete and another guy had silently walked through the gate and quickly continued on their way. Cathy was like a school girl, tapping me and mouthing, "Debbi! There he is! Pete is already here!" It was getting real. I was led onto a long and winding sidewalk that would take us to our meeting room. I had gone back into that "protective bubble" space that I mentioned experiencing after Eric's death. It's a bit of a dissociative dream-like state, but it feels like a safe and trust-worthy gift from God when feeling overwhelmed is threatening to overtake me.

Finally, I entered the room where I would meet the man I once considered a monster. I could never have imagined I would end up here back in 1991 or 2001 or 2011 or even 2021. So many years had passed, and I had an unusual confidence that this meeting would confirm that "the monster" was a man who was worthy of love, worthy of forgiveness, and worthy of my kindness.

The room looked like a glorified mobile-home office. There were two conference tables and they were arranged in a "T" formation. There were seven people in the room in addition to me (including Cathy and those I now can speculate were probably there out of curiosity). Everyone was sitting facing the same direction and I walked to the opposite end, as far away from them as I could be. I did not face them, instead I faced the empty chair where it was implied Pete would sit.

When Pete walked in, I didn't wait for anyone to say anything. Was there air in the room? I don't know. I walked over to shake his hand, and I was once again reminded of this man's incredible size. My hand disappeared into his, and it reminded me of the pictures I would take of tiny baby's hands when placed inside their parents' hands. We sat down knee-to-knee and everything I had written down flew out the window in that moment and I decided to let my heart lead the way. As far as I was concerned, there was no one else in that room except the two of us. This was happening, and it was implied the ball was in my court.

My first instinct was to get both of us breathing, so I led him through some big breaths. Breathe in. Breathe out. Breathe in. Breathe out. Just breathe.

As we exhaled the final time together I calmly said, "I'm not angry. I have forgiven you, and now it's time for you to forgive yourself."

Pete hangs his head. Shakes it gently from side to side, as if to say, "no". His demeanor is soft, humble, quiet and respectful. I know he will acquiesce to my wishes for this meeting. I know that he's doing this for me. I'm praying that my opening statement helps him to believe that this is for him too. I desired both of us to walk out of there having received what our souls needed most.

I asked him next, "What made you change your mind about meeting?"

To which he replied, "I realized that I have taken something from you that I can never give back…and I am just.so.sorry. about.that."

That would have been enough for me. We could have been done. I did not meet to evoke an apology or try to maneuver my way into one. I never thought I would hear those words, and I had intentionally denied myself from hoping for them. I was taken aback but went on.

"Tell me how you've changed over the years."

"About 10 years into my sentence, I was on the phone with my mom, and I told her I wished she would visit me more often, to which she said, 'I'm not the one who put you there, Son'. Something changed in me that day. I went back to my bunk and I began praying. I decided in that moment that I would change who I was associating with. I would no longer reduce myself to fit in and act as if my tough guy reputation with other inmates was important. It was time to grow up."

I next asked him, "What do you think would have been a fair sentence?" He had a hard time answering that, and I understand there is no right answer. I tried to ease his mind by saying, "You know. I've had a lot of time to consider that. You could have received the death penalty, and I would have been invited to watch your execution, and it wouldn't have changed a thing. Eric would still be gone and I would still be suffering, but you wouldn't be anymore. I would still be bitter, this meeting wouldn't have taken place, and your death would not have accomplished a thing."

He responded appropriately with silence and I decided to move along.

"I understand you are married and you have a daughter." He smiled sweetly and said, "And a grandson." Gulp.

"When you took Eric away from me, you took away my opportunity to be a grandmother, and I blame you for that."

No excuses. No defenses.

"Jason started using drugs when Eric was still missing. He has used for most of his life, and I blame you for that."

No excuses. No defenses.

"In a moment of time, you changed my life and my family's lives forever. We took on a life sentence too! But you know, I could be angry and bitter, and it would have cost me even more, and that would have been my own fault, my own choice. My husband and I are still married because we have God in our lives, and we decided we would not be a statistic. Our life has not been easy, and it's more than most couples could withstand. We have done it with a big, gaping wound to overcome. We just celebrated 52 years of marriage."

I looked up while I was talking about me and Paul, and what I saw was this big man's chest directly in front of me. Before I made eye contact, I noticed there were still creases in his brand-new shirt. Something in my heart flip flopped in that moment. I felt respected and honored because I knew it was a special purchase that he had made just for this meeting. I also felt God's love pouring through me toward him. Those crease lines were endearing, and although I know he didn't, it felt like he left them there for me. I was reminded that at one time or another we are all vulnerable and that our vulnerability can be a blessing to others, even when we don't plan for that or expect it.

Moving along…I reiterated that without Jesus in our lives, our marriage would have crumbled. I asked Pete, "Do you consider yourself a Christian?" I asked him this question specifically because he had mentioned praying earlier, and because I wanted to make sure he had the opportunity to hear more about Jesus if he didn't know Him yet. He didn't seem so certain. Again, this may have felt like a trick question, and I wasn't trying to set him up. I was just being blunt and asking all the questions that were bottled up within me for so long.

"Have you ever actually prayed a prayer to invite Jesus into your life to forgive you of your sins? You know you don't have to carry that weight. He will take it from you. Would you like to do that now?"

We both bowed our heads, and I led Pete through the sinner's prayer. There was a moment of levity when I prayed for "Pete". I began to thank God for Pete and for bringing Pete here to meet with me and all the sudden I burst out, "OH MY GOSH! I'M SO SORRY! IS IT OK IF I CALL YOU PETE? I ALWAYS HAVE AND OLD HABITS ARE HARD TO BREAK!" He smiled and chuckled like, "Lady, you can call me whatever you want."

I proceeded to pray with Pete, as if it were just the two of us in that room, but I had "accidentally" and shamelessly witnessed to an additional seven people that day, because we had a silent audience.

"In Jesus' name. Amen."

"In Jesus' name. Amen."

After we prayed, I reached into my bag and pulled out a brand new Bible. I faced it toward him and slid it across the table. Then I bent down and picked up a second one. It was pink, and it was for his wife. He sincerely said, "Thank you, we will keep these right on our nightstands," to which I replied, "To tell you the truth, I would rather you read them until the pages fall out." He nodded in agreement and I think he understood (at least to some degree) that we were here in this moment, doing the impossible, because of the promises in that book.

And with that, we were done. I looked at him and said, "I'm done. Are you done? Are we good?" He confirmed that we had done what we came to do. I stood up and shook his hand and said thank you for this. I knew it had required a lot of bravery on his part, and I knew he came to that meeting braced to handle anything I dished out.

The room came back into focus and the bubble dissipated. I had no idea how long we had been there. I looked at the clock and realized that time had stood still for only 30 minutes. Whether or not we knew all along, for nearly 34 years, both of our souls had waited for this 30 minutes when we would finally set each other free.

Speaking of freedom.

Eric was the first of us to receive freedom. Free from the trials of this world and of human life. He's freely worshiping Jesus, joining a chorus that echoes in eternity. Although I still have things to do on this earth, I dream of our reunion.

Pete is free. Free to be part of society. To work and to have a family. He is redeemed, set free by paying a price. He is free to reach out to me if he needs prayer or advice. He is released from worrying about my heart toward him. I pray he embraces his freedom and soars. My heartfelt prayer is that the second half of his life is full of joy and prosperity.

And praise God I am free. No longer tethered to anger, hatred or pain that held me back for years. I've forgiven the "unforgivable" and made a friend of my enemy after enduring trials no parent should ever experience. And now my final act of freedom? I've told my story. It's a record for our family and hopefully a gift for anyone who is hurting.

Reader, whoever it is you need to forgive, it is your path to freedom. Ask God to help you. Ask Him to give you supernatural assistance to do the strange, unthinkable, unusual and hardest work you will ever consider. You don't have to be enslaved to your pain. Peace is waiting.

"It is for freedom that Christ has set us free. Stand firm, then, and do not let yourselves be burdened again by a yoke of slavery." *Galatians 5:1 NIV*

11

Absolute Discharge

OVER A YEAR has passed since that day. I've continued processing the aftermath of the meeting from a place of peace and reflection. As I mentioned at the beginning of the book, I'm getting older now, and I have "nothing but time" to think about the unusual life I have had. So many difficulties, so many blessings, so incredibly grateful for it all because it's formed me, matured me, and grown me in my faith. I trust in God because He has proven Himself faithful time and time again. Being a Christian does not mean you won't have hardships. This world is full of them. It means that you have a comforter through them and you understand that this earth and the trials here are temporary. Heaven is waiting.

Pete and I are friends on Facebook. Occasionally he will reach out on holidays to say Happy Mother's Day or "please wish Paul a Happy Father's Day" or to comment on a post I've made about my child in Heaven. He is always so appropriate and cautious with his word choices, and I know his intentions are pure.

I invited Pete to contribute to this book and he didn't respond to the request, which I respect. I do pray if he ever reads this book, that he feels proud of who he's become and in no way shamed by anything I said here. I know he is also a writer, and perhaps he has a book of his own brewing in his heart. There was a point that I thought staying in close contact with Pete would be comforting for me. As strange as it sounds, because he was the last person to see Eric alive, I was hoping he would meet a need for me. I wanted to hang on to anything or anyone with any connection to Eric. I've come to terms with the fact that I would rather Jesus comfort me and Pete live in peace than hold on tightly. One day I was talking with Jason about this very topic and he said, "Mom. He's done everything you have asked of him. If it were me, and you kept asking more of me it would make me angry. You can't keep adding conditions." And Jason was right. He usually is. Sporadic contact is appropriate, and I do have warm feelings when Pete shows up in my life, but I leave it on his terms.

That being said, there will be another absolute discharge hearing in the future. I will be notified, and I will be there, and I will be offered the opportunity to share, as always. I think the depths of my healing can be illustrated with one simple statement to the judges:

Thirty four years ago I wanted this man locked up and the key thrown away. He was given a 25-to-life sentence, and I vowed that I would fight against his parole with every ounce of my energy if that time ever came. When I learned he had been released, it was three months after the parole hearing. I do believe it was a divine circumstance that I neglected to update my address with Victim's Services, and didn't know about that hearing in order to attend it. A few years later, by the time he requested "absolute discharge," I had forgiven him so thoroughly that I told the judges I didn't care whether he received it or not because I wasn't attending the hearing to speak out on that. The decision was out of my hands and I had only one request…to meet with him in person, which I believed would provide the closure we both deserved. When Pete was denied absolute discharge it allowed me to pursue our meeting through Victim's Services and eventually to fulfill my desire for reconciliation. On August 19th, 2023 Pete and I met face-to-face and I can only explain that my heart went out to him in a way that is unnatural. It is supernatural. I knew on THAT day, that someday THIS day would come, and I have been waiting for it. I am here today to speak on behalf of my son's killer. He is a changed man. He has done everything he was asked and more. He is proof that for those who want it, rehabilitation is possible. He deserves to put all of his past including the shame and stigma associated with it behind him. I want nothing more than this man to live in peace and freedom, and I do hope that he will receive absolute discharge today. Thank you.

Dearest Reader,

I believe you picked this book up for a reason. And I wrote it for a very specific reason. The story of Eric's murder is salacious and devastating but God "works all things together for good, for those who love Him and are called according to his purposes." Even murder. Even heartache. Even pain so deep we can't find a label for it.

And we know that in all things God works for the good of those who love Him, who have been called according to His purpose. Romans 8:28

If there's one thing I know, it's that God's love and care and His presence were the only reassurances that I would make it through my tragedy in one piece. If you are grieving a loss or need to forgive, He is ready and waiting to help you too. The Bible says we can "cast all our cares upon Him." All our cares!

Cast all your anxiety on Him because He cares for you. 1 Peter 4:7 NIV

If you have never invited Him into your life, here is a simple prayer that will open the door and allow Him in. After you pray, look for a local church that teaches from the Bible and immerse yourself. God's word is living and active and it will change you!

Dear Jesus,

My hurt is overwhelming and my heart needs put back together. I don't have the ability to do this alone, I need your help. Forgive me for making choices that take me further from you and further from your plans for my life. Help me connect with the right resources to lead and guide me in becoming the woman/ man that you created me to be. Teach me your ways and set me free from anything holding me back. Thank you Jesus, for dying on the cross so that I may truly live.

Amen

<h1 style="text-align:center">Epilogue</h1>

IT WAS OCTOBER of 2025, and this book was done, until it wasn't. We had just passed the rough draft off to a couple of trusted friends, asking them to look for mistakes we may have missed. Final edits. The plan was to then "put a bow on it" and begin looking into publishing. I secretly hoped that Pete would respond to my March 2nd message when I told him I was writing the book…but over seven months had passed, and I hadn't heard anything back from him. I really wanted him to understand my intentions. I had no plans to exploit or embarrass him, and I would keep the focus on redemption and hope. I had chased communication with him for so long in the past, and I vowed to never do that again. Although I wanted his "blessing" before moving forward with the project, I didn't need his permission.

But God.

He sure does have a sense of humor.

I don't know why I think my life will ever be ordinary. The twists and turns still take me by surprise.

October 14th, 2025, I received this message, out of the blue:

Dear Mrs. Edwards,

I pray that my words find you well. I wanted to take this moment to say that I am grateful to you for your strength, your faith, and the standard that you have instilled in me. There are no words to make up for what I have done, and I fear that I may never be able to forgive myself as you have forgiven me, but I can say that you have become someone I never wish to disappoint. I pray that you and your family are well. I thank you from the bottom of my heart for everything that you helped change in my life. And if you ever wish to meet again, it would sincerely be my pleasure to do so. I am absolutely humbled by you, Mrs. Edwards. Thank you.

Come again?

Yes. My answer is yes. My answer is yes to love. Yes to connection. Yes to friendship. Yes to peace. Yes to unity. Yes to building bridges. Yes to healing. Yes to meeting. My answer is enthusiastically, YES!

I called my collaborative writer, Shannon, and announced, "GOD IS ON THE MOVE! WE ARE GOING TO TUCSON TO MEET WITH PETE. THIS BOOK NEEDS AN EPILOGUE!" I knew she would agree because we had been on the last 10 months of this crazy ride together.

We booked a hotel for November 15th, found a restaurant that looked like a nice place to stay and visit for a while, made the arrangements…and then…we waited and prayed. Waiting and praying should be easy for me by now, I have spent my whole life waiting and praying, but I have to admit that quieting my mind remains a challenge and is a discipline that even "older saints" like me are still perfecting.

November 15th finally came and Shannon and I checked into our hotel a little early to drop our things off, regroup, and pray. We prayed that the Holy Spirit would go before us and occupy the table ahead of us. We prayed that God would prepare our hearts, individually and collectively. Mostly we prayed that Pete and his wife (Pamela) would feel God's love flowing between us and covering us. We were ready. Apprehensive, excited, anxious, every emotion was swirling within us as we pulled into Amelia's Mexican Kitchen at 2 pm.

Pete and Pamela pulled into the parking lot just ahead of us and I quickly (as quickly as my body moves these days) jumped out to greet them. Pamela rushed over to hug me, and Pete was right behind. He leaned down and hugged me too, and I was so glad he broke the ice.

Introductions were made, and we were seated quickly. Conversation flowed easily and there was nothing awkward or uncomfortable between us. Pete and I sat across from one another, and Shannon and Pamela did the same.

We talked about everything and anything. I didn't want to shy away from saying hard things, and I won't ever shy away from speaking Eric's name. But beyond that, we talked about babies and grandbabies. We talked about hobbies (Pete likes plants, and is a fan of the Mexican pottery stores for which Tucson is famous). We discussed recipes, and how he and Pamela met. We talked a lot about this book and redemption and how "crazy" this meet up actually was. The concept of forgiveness isn't crazy. The embracing of it - fully without limits - is the crazy thing. This is what forgiveness is supposed to be, but it takes maturity, humility, and a willingness to take a risk on being hurt, again.

Meeting Pamela and seeing Pete with a wife he clearly adores was precious. She is precious. I was watching their body language with each other. There are people who would say Pete's transformation is "faked", but there is nothing that could convince me of that. I noticed how patient, gentle and kind he was toward his wife. I saw the love, so evident between them, and I marveled at the story of their meeting and how "Pamela asked Pete to marry her". They both blushed and acknowledged she wasn't going to let him go. This just can't be faked.

Pete had much to share about his personal journey as well, and his wisdom is astounding. He shared that he had helped 500 young men get their GED's in prison. He shared that he carries around an invisible backpack of bricks. It's heavy, and it's full of his regrets. Sometimes he gets to symbolically remove a brick and lighten his load, but it's his backpack to carry, and he will continue to do that as long as there are bricks still in it. He tilts his head, thinks hard for a moment, and asks, "Which is more important: What we do know, or what we don't know yet?" He's committed to life-long learning and growth. Pamela is quietly cheering him on as he spills wisdom that only a man who has reflected deeply on the meaning of everything, can do. He stated several times that he did not want to be a disappointment to me. There were not enough words to convince him he is not a disappointment, but an inspiration. Tears were flowing when Eric was mentioned and he said, "Debbi. I will spend the rest of my life honoring the life of that young man." In that moment, Eric was real again. That was a gift.

When it was "my turn," I assured him that I know Eric is fine. Better than fine. I'm fine. With every ounce of me, I want him to be fine too. I said, "You are forgiven! But you won't be able to forgive yourself if you don't let go of shame!" He acknowledges this is a struggle. I reiterated that I'm in support of absolute discharge. We discussed it a bit, and I offered to do anything I can to help that process. Pete says, "This book could be helpful." We gave him a copy of the manuscript and told him that we want him to be proud of it. He was gracious to accept it and said, "I'm going to start reading this tonight."

It was time to end our visit. Shannon asked Pete if she could get a picture of us together, making sure to qualify, "If you don't want the picture shown, shared or printed, we will honor that. It's totally up to you." He reassured her there is no problem with sharing the photos. Pamela said she was hoping we would get some pictures as well, and we got some fantastic shots. As strange as it sounds, I love the photos where Pete is towering over me. "A gentle giant" describes him perfectly.

Our meeting ended with heart-felt goodbyes and "until we meet again." And, we will meet again. We are both determined to take what happened on December 4th, 1991 and redeem it. We refuse to be defined by tragedy or to allow the enemy's plan of division and heartache to rule over us. Me and my friend Pete? We are more than conquerors, and our story will help change lives. We shuffled into the parking lot, promised to stay in touch (I believe it!) and hugged one another all around. Pamela pulled me close and whispered in my ear, "Thank you for forgiving him." People who refuse to forgive are missing out on so much. To God be the glory!

"People change." It's true. But sometimes when they change for good I think they are finally allowing themselves to settle into who they always were, deep down inside. Dropping our walls, losing the false personas we've created from a place of pain or immaturity (or for self-preservation) reveals who we really are and who we were created to be. In Pete's case, I think a kind and gentle soul was always inside, and I'm so glad I got to meet him.

Our hearts were full when we drove home the next day, November 16th. It was the 7th anniversary of Pete's release, which was ironic. And on this beautiful Sunday afternoon, it was raining, just like it was that December day in 1991 when I just knew the rain represented God grieving along with me. As Shannon and I traveled the peaceful road between Tucson and Queen Creek, we noted the rare beauty of a desert rain. She leaned over and said, "It's raining, Debbi. Even God is crying today. But this time, it's tears of joy".

He has shown you, O man, what is good; And what does the Lord require of you but to do justly, to love mercy, and to walk humbly with your God? Micah 6:8 NIV

Discussion Questions
Part 4

1. Why do you think Pete backed out of the first meeting with Debbi? What do you suspect he was feeling about the meeting?

2. Did Pete's demeanor when the meeting began surprise you? What did you notice most as Debbi described him physically as well as behaviorally?

3. Debbi takes a "motherly tone" with Pete at times? What seems to be his response to her in those moments?

4. Debbi says "waiting and praying" are hard for her, even as an "older saint". What does this tell you about our journey with Jesus? Do we ever stop growing in Him? Where is He stretching you now?

5. When Debbi traveled to Tucson for the second time, to meet with Pete (and Pamela) in an informal setting, what about that meeting surprised you? Do you think they will stay in touch for a lifetime?

About Shannon Musa

SHANNON MUSA WAS raised in Mesa, Arizona and has lived in Queen Creek, Arizona for most of her adult life. She is "solar powered" and loves hiking, paddle boarding, a good (paperback!) book while floating in the pool, and being outdoors as much as possible.

Shannon has been married for 25 years to her husband, Tim, and they have two teenage sons together. When they aren't doing yardwork or attending their children's many events, you can find them at one of the local coffee shops, where they are surely planning their next beach vacation.

Shannon was interested in helping Debbi write her story because of her personal connection to it. Not only was she a friend of Eric's, she had heard Debbi tell her story as they crossed paths at church events over the years. Shannon's mission is to help Debbi's story reach everyone who needs to hear a powerful testimony of mercy's triumph over justice.

Contact us for speaking engagement information, special orders, or general inquiries.

Our authors can be reached at:
justiceandmercybook@gmail.com

Debbi and Pete November 15, 2025